MW00587164

Praise for
The Incredible State of Absolute Nothingness

"*The Incredible State of Absolute Nothingness* is the work of a contemporary spiritual master, one of those extremely gifted mystics that comes along maybe once in a generation."

John Paul Gunn
President, Meditativeminds.com

"This book has a presence, it has an effect – perhaps the best way to describe it is that it is 'psychoactive.' The X on the cover is very powerful indeed."

John N. Inglis
Artist & Author, *In Quest of a Countenance*

"*The Incredible State of Absolute Nothingness* is a fascinating read. Stephen D'Amico's journey has intersected with practically every spiritual technology and category out there. Read it and find out how deep the human mind can go. This is a rare and wonderful book!"

Jeff Warren
Author, *The Head Trip*

"I highly recommend this book if you're interested in reading about the journey to Enlightenment by a true spiritual teacher. It radiates spiritual energy to the reader from the pages."

Claire Elek
Visual Artist & Activist

"A truly fascinating and honest account of a life affected deeply by Spirit. The descriptive language that Stephen has so eloquently honed helps to unfold this autobiographical journey in ways that transcend many other accounts of enlightenment I've read."

Carson Foster
Founder, Viewniverse.com

"This book gives some very clear signposts for those of us on the spiritual path. I've read many of the same insights elsewhere; however, Stephen has integrated all these insights as different aspects or stages of one spiritual journey, which is amazing. I'm sure the world will benefit from this book."

Dashen Kamalanathan
Coordinator, Zeitgeist Toronto

Praise for
Stephen D'Amico

"Stephen D'Amico is one of a refreshing new breed of spiritual teachers and guides whose personal breakthrough represents an extraordinary state of permanent nondual awareness that his ordinary humanity shows is an increasingly accessible stage of human evolution for us all. When it comes to moving past the psychological and emotional obstacles on our path, his work represents another evolutionary breakthrough. Rather than allow us to stay 'organized around the wound' in the name of healing on the one hand, or foster a 'spiritual bypass operation' that disregards our human development on the other, the laserlike clarity of his consciousness penetrates the egoic mist, no matter how thick, and then lets it naturally dissolve and lift in the clear light of awareness. No matter where you are on your journey of awakening, I recommend Stephen as a professional guide for the kind of grounded soul work that has become so urgent in our increasingly polarized world."

Cedric Speyer
Clinical Supervisor, Shepell.fgi

"Stephen is a man who has done an incredible amount of personal and spiritual work. Because of this, he operates at a very high level of vibration. Things often become clearer just by being in his presence."

Bonnie Pedota
Author & Spiritual Psychotherapist

"Stephen's presence alone was enough to trigger my own discovery of True Nature, and I would recommend his acquaintance to anyone serious about self-realization and its human actualization."

Neil Jalaldeen
Guide, Liberation Unleashed

"Stephen emanates peace, consciousness and presence!"

Katia Millar
Founder, Positive Fabulous Women

"In my 25 years of investigations and studies on human evolution and esoteric spirituality, I've met more than ten enlightened teachers and find Stephen's message to be both universal and unique. We are blessed to have his compassionate wisdom accessible."

Sara MacHin
Holistic Lifestyle Consultant & Yoga Instructor

"I've met many spiritual leaders, and I have no doubt that Stephen is not working from within the confines of the ego. His gentle nature and open-heartedness are both apparent. I believe any work he does is for the betterment of humanity."

Dee Dussault
Founder, Follow Your Bliss

"I am a scientist and have been on the spiritual path for over 30 years. I feel fortunate to have met Stephen. His teachings articulate the nature of the spiritual path with depth and clarity. People travel to the Himalayas to find a Master; here we have One in Toronto!"

Dilip Kumar
Managing Director, MD Group

"I have noticed much clarity occurs in any encounter where Stephen D'Amico is present. He is unshakable in his conviction about what happened during his awakening and it seems to inform his every moment. He appears to have little or no neurosis, and is ever ready, calm, and open as far as I can tell. It is without words that Stephen does much of his work. And his work is to wake us up, to humbly reveal what he has found. Like all the great teachers, he simply wants to bring relief and is excited to let us know about something beautiful and real that is available here and now."

Gary Justice
Music Producer & Meditation Teacher

The Incredible State of Absolute Nothingness

A Personal Account of Spiritual Enlightenment

Stephen D'Amico

AMEEK
PRESS

Credits

This book was made with help from the following people: Aron Szocs rendered the image on the front cover using Photoshop. Sameer Haque helped finish the cover design in the same program. Cameron MacMaster took the portrait photograph. Several pictures inside were prepared for print by Gabriel Dumitriu and Javier A. Romo. The final two photographs were taken by John Ribeiro and Garo Karaoghlanian. The chakra illustration on page 136 was reproduced with permission by Gemisphere. Deanna Figueiredo elicited voice recordings used for the initial phase of writing. Sumaiya Matin, Jamie Yamashita, and Gita Ramchandani transcribed those audio files into text. Sue Deacon and Aniko Szocs provided valuable editorial suggestions throughout the writing process. Many other friends and colleagues helped with revisions. The layout was done using OpenOffice. The typeface is Palatino with Optima. Both fonts were designed by Hermann Zapf. The Palatino font employs a strong, open style that's highly legible, and the graceful curves of the Optima font give a clear impression to the eye. Happy reading!

Reader Advisory

Reading this book can be highly transformative, whether you are ready or not. As the author and publisher, I cannot be held accountable for the dissolution of readers' egos or any other changes in consciousness arising from or connected to the use of the information contained in this book. People with a history of mental illness, severe trauma, or panic disorder are urged not to use the techniques in this book without a qualified guide. If you decide to try them, you agree to absolve me, Stephen D'Amico, the author and publisher, of any responsibility for their application or misapplication.

Library and Archives Canada Cataloguing in Publication

D'Amico, Stephen, 1973-, author
The incredible state of absolute nothingness : a personal account of spiritual enlightenment / Stephen D'Amico.

Includes bibliographical references.
ISBN 978-0-9738010-1-9 (pbk.)
1. D'Amico, Stephen, 1973-. 2. Spiritual life. 3. Spirituality. I. Title.
BL64.D286 2013   204'.2   C2013-903302-5

Because of Your Mysterious Origin & Your
Bewildering Infinity. Because of Your Formless
Essence & Your Eternal Consciousness. Because of
Your Boundless Being & Your Neverending Bliss.

Because of
Your
Cosmic
Light

**ALL GLORY
GOES TO GOD**

& Your
Mani-
festing
Energy.

Because of Your Electric Heartbeat & Your
Oscillating Hum. Because of Your Almighty Power
& Your Amazing Creation. Because of Your
Indivisible Unity & Your Interwoven Variety.
Because of Your Magnetic Attraction & Your
Exquisite Symmetry. Because of Your Invisible
Immanence & Your Revealing Activity. Because of
Your Perpetual Appearance & Your Sorcerous
Vanishing. Because of Your Visionary Dreaming &
Your Magical Animation. Because of Your Dynamic
Ordering & Your Total Care. Because of Your
Generous Spirit & Your Outstanding Patience.
Because of Your Ultimate Goodness & Your Infallible
Justice. Because of Your Supreme Knowing & Your
Loving Grace. Because of Your Compassionate Mercy
& Your Abounding Kindness. Because of Your
Synchronistic Guidance & Your Timely Blessings.
Because of Your Transcendental Knowing & Your
Optimizing Intelligence. Because of Your Illuminat-
ing Truth & Your Liberating Wisdom. Because of
Your Entrancing Awareness & Your Elevating Gaze.
Because of Your Bottomless Depths & Your
Unshakeable Grounding. Because of Your Unlimited
Widening & Your Centering Core. Because of Your
Epic Equanimity & Your Endless Joy.

Table of Contents

Introduction

WHEN I WAS 22, I went through a complete spiritual transformation that led to a permanent realization of my **true nature**. On the night it happened, I was lying in my bed when my awareness suddenly expanded, sort of like a camera panning outwards until it travels beyond the edge of space and time. Except in my case, I felt myself merge with this infinite spaciousness. Merge and stay. Permanently.

For the next few years, I lived in a totally transcendent but also perfect state of contentment. The easiest way to convey this change is with another analogy. After this transformation, I felt like a puppet master, directing the action down below, but no longer actually inhabiting my body. As liberating as this period was, I eventually came back down into the world and got re-embodied.

This book is a detailed account of that overall process, as well as an autobiography of my entire life so far, beginning with some of my earliest memories and mystical experiences. Many of the events are quite extraordinary and may challenge the reader's skepticism. All I can say is that I've written about my life as straightforwardly as possible to document my journey before, during, and after **enlightenment**.

Because this book is as much about my personal journey as it is about the nature of the spiritual path, some readers may wonder how accurate the information is. This is one of the biggest challenges when writing about spirituality: how to distinguish what is absolute or objectively true from what is subjective or relative.

I'm aware that my individual consciousness or **soul** has influenced the way I've experienced many of these events, but I'm equally aware that a much larger mystical reality girds my personal journey.

How do I know? William James, one of the great fathers of modern psychology and mystical experience, called it the *noetic* aspect of knowledge. This is a mode of knowing that works with the mind's eye and provides an inherent kind of certainty that is the **phenomenological** foundation of mysticism. Basically, once you're plugged in, it has more authority than any scripture from any tradition, although parallels can often be found for added confirmation, which is something I have done in this book.

Part of my reason for doing so is to provide some extra context and external validation for my experiences. But more importantly, matching my experiences with the same or similar ones found in the spiritual literature of the world demonstrates that there is a common thread of mystical wisdom and universal truth that recurs in every epoch and culture, something known as the **perennial philosophy**.

One of my purposes for writing this book is to share some of this knowledge using my experience of enlightenment and attainment of **self-realization** as an opportunity to do so. Connected with this intention is an even more important function of this book, which is dedicated to facilitating this same awakening in the reader. To that end, I have included a handful of simple and effective techniques for you to try that I discovered during my childhood or later on. Plus, I encourage you to emulate any of the other spiritual activities I engaged in on my path, which you'll come across as you read about my journey. And, finally, I hope that my unfolding will arouse your own **inner guide**, so that you can find your unique way on the path of awakening and enlightenment.

Also, the descriptions of my spiritual experiences in this book were written from the same states of consciousness being described. Words that are written from a particular state of spiritual realization have the power to awaken the same state of realization in the reader. In other words, this book can help transform your consciousness just by reading it, as long as you're open to receiving this kind of awakening transmission through the written word.

Reading this book can assist you in one more important way. It can help you to see where you're at in your own journey. Think of it as a tool for orientation. Right now you may be at one of these three stages on the spiritual path: aspiring to make contact with your **higher self**, realizing this transcendent dimension of being that unites us all, or returning to your body to live as a self-realized human being in the world.

Strap yourself in. Here we go.

My earliest memory of a divine reality was of a subtle vision that arose in my mind's eye every night before falling asleep...I can even recall it happening as a baby.

Chapter 1

Incarnating and a Recurring Metamorphosis

F ALLING. That was the sensation I felt as I left the formless
dimension for the world of form. Prior to the moment of
incarnating, I was looking down into a funnel of diminishing
consciousness, knowing that it was time for me to choose my
parents. I was attracted to the presence of two souls perfectly
suited to become my mother and father because they each possessed specific qualities that I knew would help me awaken in
this lifetime.

From the soul of the man I chose to be my father, I saw
that I would inherit his extraordinary ability to persevere.
And from the soul of the woman I chose to be my mother, I
saw that I would acquire her undogmatic view of life. It was
clear to me that the combination of these qualities would ensure my ability to rediscover the formless dimension I was
about to leave behind. The last impression I have is the sensation of falling, which felt similar to passing out.

This memory of incarnating came back to me during the
spiritual transformation I underwent in 1996. I was twenty-
two years old at the time.

Going back as far as I can remember, my earliest memory
of a divine reality involved a subtle vision that arose in my
mind's eye every night before falling asleep. Soon after closing my eyes, my attention would gravitate towards the middle of my forehead, the location of the *ajna* or brow **chakra**,
which opens the mind's eye (also called the *inner* or *third eye*).
As mine did, the following transformations of consciousness
would unfold.

Peering steadily into the formlessness of pure consciousness, a tiny point of light about the same size and brightness
as a star would appear. This luminous sphere would emerge

from beyond the outermost edge of my awareness, growing bigger and brighter as it drew closer. Before long, it looked a lot like an incandescent light bulb.

This glowing globe would then pause in the center of my consciousness while I admired its beautiful brilliance. It had the same pearly golden sheen as the surface of the sun without the blinding quality of physical sunlight.

Eventually, I'd feel an overwhelming desire to move towards this luminous form. Responding to my intention, the shining sphere would continue expanding, slowly swelling in size until it filled the surrounding space of my awareness.

Soon, the light was no longer an object in my mind's eye. Instead, my entire being was filled with light, at which point I was no longer in my body. The boundary of my being expanded beyond it and merged with an infinite realm made of this spiritual light.

Once inside this cosmic dimension, I saw and felt what it was made of. It was fluidic with zillions of sparkling tendrils that kept sprouting out of the gloriously gleaming liquid and networking with each other in incalculable ways with mind boggling speed and precision.

As this was happening, I had the clear sense that what I was observing was operating on a transcendental plane of reality – a place where anything and everything is possible, and where all conceivable contraries are instantly reconciled.

The sensation of dwelling *in* and *as* this superconscious substance was blissful beyond measure. I looked forward to experiencing it every night. I couldn't wait to close my eyes in preparation for sleep knowing that I'd get to merge with this dazzling metaphysical dimension once again. But the next phase of these nightly journeys led to another dimension that was far less desirable.

Eventually, the limitless luminosity would begin shrinking, and along with it, so would the boundary of my being. It was like the energy that sustained this golden radiance was on a dimmer switch that slowly got turned down. As it lost its power, the light became visible as a sphere in my mind's eye again. However, when it reappeared, something was different. Something I'd always hoped wouldn't happen.

The once perfectly immaculate sphere was covered with what looked like sunspots. It was clear that these dark blemishes were symptoms of a much deeper infection, which manifested as gnarly roots growing beneath the surface down to the very core of the golden orb.

I knew that these roots would eventually take over and completely extinguish the light, and that there was nothing I could do to stop this from happening. There was a way to restore the untainted light, but it required engaging in the next part of this process, which I always resisted.

If I wanted to enjoy the higher plane of boundless light again, I had to let the infestation take over and turn the golden orb into an infinitesimally small mass of tangled roots. Then, I would have to become one with this decaying dot in order to reverse the process and restore the pristine light.

I always tried to stall this part of the journey. I didn't want to go through the shrinking phase because I was afraid that I, too, would shrivel up and disappear into oblivion. At the same time, on a deeper level, I knew that this was unlikely to happen. I had gone through this metamorphosis every night as far back as I could remember, so I was quite familiar with the procedure from beginning to end.

As a result, I knew that both *points* on either side of this inner trip – the contracting dot of decay and the expanding spark of light – worked together to facilitate a much larger process that was at work. Still, this foreknowledge or understanding didn't make the journey any less striking each time, nor did it diminish the dread I felt while going through the shrinking phase.

Inevitably, there would come a point when every last lingering glow of light would disappear. At that point, I knew I had no other choice except to stop resisting and let go. As soon as I did, my consciousness shrank in size, reducing the boundary of my entire being to a tiny point before disappearing.

For a brief moment, all sense of having a self ceased to exist. It was like a gap – a cessation of existence – without my actually falling asleep or becoming totally unconscious. But this state of non-existence was only temporary. The very next moment I would recognize that this formless dimension was the actual essence of my true nature. And once I was back in touch with this original state of being, I would either wait for the light to return, or go to sleep. If I chose to repeat the process, the point of light would re-emerge.

Like blowing on a dying ember so it starts glowing bright white again, a seemingly invisible force would re-energize the infected dot and turn it back into a starlike point of light. This luminous point would continue expanding as before, simultaneously widening the dimensions of my being until I was basking in the boundless light again.

I went through this metamorphosis at least once every night, but more often than not, I would go through the entire process several times, allowing my being to expand and contract repeatedly. At a certain point, usually when I was ready to fall asleep, I would intentionally stop the process.

In order to do so, I would let the mottled object shrink until it dissolved, which would lead to the recognition of my true nature as expected. But instead of anticipating the light to return, I would keep my attention focused on the formless essence of my own being, while deliberately sinking into the underlying emptiness, allowing myself to descend into the peaceful depths of sleep.

This went on every night for years. I can even recall it happening as a baby. What's more, as I got older, I began to understand what this nightly journey meant in a more conscious way. It mainly functioned as a way to return my soul to its original state of formlessness, but it had other important and beneficial effects.

For example, every time I fused with the shrinking mass of tangled roots, I would undergo a parallel process that integrated any lingering emotional or psychological material I had accumulated during the day. It was a kind of digestion process that metabolized any **karmic** holdings.

To understand how this happened, it is necessary to point out that this process awakened a noetic mode of knowing not available in normal experience. In this mode, it was clear to me that the roots I encountered during the contraction phase were more than some curious inner phenomenon. They were (and are) a fundamental activity of the human mind.

More specifically, these roots are actual ego structures that are made from the emotional states and mental thinking processes that go into their development. By seeing these ego structures in their fundamental form, I was able to understand how each root expressed a specific meaning that was based on how I made sense of my experiences that day. And the result of this subtle perception allowed me to assimilate all sorts of psychological and emotional material and turn it into self-knowledge at the end of every day.

This same experience provided access to other realms of knowledge, mysteries that extended beyond the inner workings of my psyche. Foremost in this regard was an under-standing of the relationship between the boundless realm of light and the original formless dimension, and how they are involved in the manifestation of reality. Stated briefly, I saw that the luminous dimension is the active counterpart need-ed for the formless dimension to manifest as everything in cre-ation, both seen and unseen. In other words, everything in ex-istence is first born in darkness and then evolves from light in a continuum of cosmic energy that creates and sustains the en-tire universe.

Going through this metamorphosis also revealed a deep-er understanding about life and death. I saw that everything in existence goes through a similar cycle of expansion and contraction. Based on this insight, I knew that death is just a transformation of one form into another, a change in the over-all pattern of the formless dimension manifesting as all forms.

As a child this was no small insight. It released me from fearing my own death and deepened my understanding that biological death is not the end of life, but rather a threshold that our evolving souls cross over from one incarnation to the next.

Another spiritual truth noetically discovered through this experience was the knowledge that the divine light emanat-ing from this supernal dimension exists even in the most un-conscious aspects of creation, which includes our lives here on Earth.

As I got older and became aware of the existence of evil in this world, I knew that the predominant force in the uni-verse is actually love, and that God only allows evil to exist as a necessary consequence of giving the ability of free will to beings like us. This insight was accompanied by the com-fort of knowing that this world is destined to become a home of love, light, and unity, which I always implicitly knew to be the true evolutionary future of humanity.

As you can see from my life, there are modes of knowing that go beyond what is considered ordinary, some of which include the emergence of *vehicles of transformation*. These are structures or subtle forms of consciousness that can facilitate various types of spiritual transformation. There are probably far more types of these vehicles than those that have been recorded by the individuals who have encountered them, but out of the collected knowledge of this mystical wisdom, it is clear that there are certain shared or universal ones.

For example, the central form that facilitated the metamorphosis I described above is known as the *divine spark* in several mystical traditions. It is most common to Gnosticism, but it is also present in Kabbalah and Sufism, among other traditions. According to these traditions, the purpose of this divine spark is to re-establish our connection with the *upper worlds* or spiritual dimensions of reality, which corresponds with my own experience. And, as I just mentioned, there are many different types of vehicles that can appear on the path. We'll explore a few more of them using examples from my journey later on.

For now, I'd like to offer a few concluding remarks on the subject of vehicles of transformation. First, it is important to mention that a common mistake is to regard them as something to be grasped at for their own sake. While an effort to expand our consciousness is necessary to elicit them in the first place, there is no guarantee that any subtle forms will appear on the path to enlightenment. So, although certain vehicles can emerge, they may not be necessary, and therefore, do not need to be sought after.

Another common mistake is to become overly attached to such phenomena if they do emerge, which actually impedes the deeper transformational processes they are intended to facilitate. In sum, all forms come and go, including mystical or visionary ones. This applies to vehicles of transformation as well, particularly after they have served their purpose, at which point they tend to disappear.

Moving on to more concrete aspects of the spiritual path, there are three qualities that are universally recognized as being indispensable for all aspirants, which were also present in my own life from an early age. They are introspection, observation, and concentration.

If we want to develop our capacity for spiritual growth, we need to cultivate our ability to observe and to recall what we have experienced. Additionally, we need to cultivate the ability to trace our psychological and emotional states back to their subconscious sources because this kind of self-analysis promotes healthy personal integration, which naturally leads to a widening in the boundary of the self beyond ego.

The exercise below will help you develop the powers of introspection and observation. It is also designed to release the wise and loving guidance of your soul, which ultimately wants nothing more than for you to fully embody and express your true nature in this lifetime.

Self-Observation
Each night before you go to sleep, spend 5–10 minutes recalling your day from start to finish. As you think about various situations, ask yourself: *How do I feel about what happened? What was good? What was not so good? If I could revisit this situation again, what would I do differently?* Reflect on any associated thoughts and insights that arise. The idea is to bring everyday situations into your awareness and observe them in a mindful way. Doing so releases the liberating wisdom of your soul.

The other ability necessary for making progress on the spiritual path is to cultivate the powers of concentration. This entails focusing attention in a sustained way. An exercise to do so is described in the shaded box below.

> *Focusing Attention*
> Cultivating focused attention, also known as making the mind one-pointed, involves focusing on an object of meditation in a sustained way. Traditionally, either the tip of a candle flame or a black dot drawn on a white background is recommended. Gazing at the dot in the center of the X on the cover of this book will also work. Start with 15–20 seconds first, then 30–40 seconds, then 1–2 minutes, gradually increasing the amount of time with practice until you can sustain your attention for 5–10 minutes, followed by longer periods if you like.

In addition to honing your ability to concentrate, sustaining your attention in this way can help develop your ability to move progressively deeper into the formless depths of being using another method I'd like to share with you that employs the focal point of attention to reach the **nondual** core of being. I call this method *tracing back the witness*, which I'll expand upon in chapter three, along with two other useful methods. In the next chapter, I'd like to provide a brief history of my life, starting with my birth.

Chapter 2

A Brief History of My Life

I WAS BORN ON SEPTEMBER 19ᵀᴴ, 1973, at Mount Sinai Hospital in Toronto. According to my mother, I was an "unfussy" baby. I hardly ever cried and usually slept so soundly that she would often have to check in on me just to make sure I was still breathing.

The delivery, in contrast, was a tougher job. My mother was in labor for almost twenty-four hours. The early stages were easy. Her contractions were mild and infrequent right up until her cervix was fully dilated. But for some reason, I wasn't dropping through the birth canal.

The obstetrician decided to induce labor by breaking the waters, a medical practice that involves deliberately rupturing the amniotic sac. My mother describes the remaining thirty minutes it took to finally deliver me as the most excruciating pain she has ever experienced.

There is some mixed ancestry in my family tree, beginning with my parents, who coincidentally share the same root name, Val. My father, whose first name is Valentino, was born in Italy and emigrated to Canada when he was five. And my mother, whose first name is Valerie, was born in Britain and emigrated to Canada when she was seven.

My maternal grandparents were also from different ethnic backgrounds. My grandfather was born and raised in Newfoundland, and my grandmother was originally from Britain. They met and married during World War II, while my grandfather was stationed in Britain as an Allied serviceman. Although it was never confirmed as factual by anyone in the family, my grandfather claimed that one of his ancestors was the Chief of a Mi'kmaq tribe, a First Nations people from the Maritime region of Canada.

My paternal grandparents share the same ethnic origins. They both came from a mountainous region in Italy known as Molise. My grandmother came from a small village called Cantalupo, which had a population of less than a thousand. And my grandfather was from a neighboring village called San Massimo, which was only slightly larger with a few hundred more inhabitants. Like many Italian immigrant families, their agrarian roots were so deep that even though they were employed in Canada their entire working lives, they still kept livestock and grew fruits and vegetables in their backyard.

Italian families keep track of extensive family ties, often including second, third, and even fourth cousins, so I was fortunate in the sense that I had the benefit of experiencing an extended sense of family. And although the family on my mother's side did not trace the family circle as widely, my maternal grandparents, and all my immediate aunts, uncles, and cousins were and still are closely connected. The strong family bonds on this side of the family were due, in large part, to the fact that the entire time I was growing up, we all spent summers together at a camping ground in a conservation area called Albion Hills near Bolton, Ontario.

I lived in the same house the entire time I was growing up, so I was also fortunate to know what it was like to have deep roots in more than one place. We lived in a large townhouse complex located in a municipality of Toronto called Willowdale.

Childhood home

At the time, it was part of the new suburban sprawl movement now so common in most expanding cities around the world. My parents moved into this townhouse complex when I was two years old, and we never moved or lived anywhere else the entire time I was growing up.

I am the third of four siblings. I have two older brothers and a younger sister. My second oldest brother is John, and Deanna is the name of my younger sister. My oldest brother, Michael, is actually a half brother, but we never thought of him this way. He moved out when I was quite young so, in a way, I ended up being a middle child.

As is common being a middle child, I was often overlooked and had to settle for less. Admittedly, this was due, in part, to having a quieter, less demanding nature than my siblings. I deliberately overlooked my own wants and needs, mainly because I was content to get by with less, but also because I didn't want to burden my parents with too many demands. Since my basic needs were usually provided for, the nature of my early life could be described as a kind of *middle*

As a young boy

way – neither feeling the sting of unfulfilled desires, nor having to suffer due to any real sense of lack.

My mother did most of the child rearing when we were young. Growing up, she was the one who was always around. Although she was almost always present physically, her consciousness was often somewhere else. She had an uncanny ability to get entranced in books and television, or lost in thought. She read constantly, often as many as two or three books a day. Her reading tastes are different now, but there was always a romance novel in her hand back then. If her mind wasn't preoccupied in some fictional fantasy life, she was usually absorbed in an old black-and-white movie on

12

TV. Otherwise, she would sit in her chair, staring off into space, lost in some reverie of the past, or engaged in some form of contemplative reflection.

I would often ask her what she was thinking about whenever I noticed she was in one of her meditative moods. I'd have to gently tap her on the knee and repeat the word *Mom* with just the right tempo and cadence in order to deftly and peacefully break her free from her inner musings. If successful, I would occasionally catch her reflecting on some aspect of her life, the details of which she would then share with me, explaining things in a way that she knew I'd understand.

My father was the exact opposite in the sense of being immersed in the physical realm, responding to the worldly demands and obligations of working to make money to provide for our family. He worked long hours and often didn't get home until quite late in the evening, usually after Deanna, John, and I had gone to bed. But if we were still awake when my father did come home, we'd all race to the front door of the house to be the first one to leap into his arms and give him a big, warm hug and kiss.

My parents argued a lot. There was also the usual arguing and fighting between us siblings, but the predominant feeling in our house was always warm and loving.

I was an active kid. I loved playing outside, usually staying out as late as possible. I hardly ever did any homework, and in class I was known for being a bit of a clown. I loved cracking jokes and making people laugh, but I was also cunning enough to avoid getting into a lot of trouble.

School wasn't challenging for me. I'd grab desks by windows and stare at the sky, watching the clouds transform into shapes to pass time. Doodling arabesques in the margins of my notebooks was another way to lose myself in patterns.

In the schoolyard, I was usually the first person to befriend the new kid to help him or her fit in faster, and I made it a personal mission to ensure that the less popular kids were never the victims of bullying.

I was an okay student, although; as I said, I rarely, if ever, did any homework. I found school boring and would often ask my mother to let me take days off, which she usually allowed within reason. To make sure I passed from one grade to the next, I would cram for tests and only complete the most important assignments. Not surprisingly, the one consistent remark on all my report cards was that I wasn't reaching my full potential as a student.

This pattern continued up until I reached grade eleven, at which point my ability to cram was no longer good enough to earn the grades I would need to enroll in university, which was something I always felt I had to do.

So, I had to start studying and doing my homework. I didn't mind, though, because I developed a newfound thirst for knowledge right around the same time.

My friends and I would get together to do our homework on a regular basis. We'd usually hang out at a local coffee shop, and once our homework assignments were completed, we'd sit around smoking cigarettes and drinking coffee, debating and discussing all sorts of ideas from our latest philosophical theories about the meaning of life to how to solve real world issues.

For a brief period, I was convinced that communism was the answer to everything. Unless I really applied myself in school, though, and worked diligently in order to get an A or A+, I remained mostly a B or B+ student, a pattern that continued right through university.

The month of my birth makes my astrological sign Virgo, and whatever you may think about this system of divination, there is no denying that I share the personality traits of this sign. Virgo individuals tend to be introverted and quiet by nature with a tendency to drop into the background.

Looking back at my early life now, I can see how the combination of these qualities helped me to stay connected to the formless dimension of being. During my childhood, I had discovered several different ways to reconnect with my true nature, and the one I used most relied on having these qualities.

I'll elaborate on this method in the next chapter. For now, it is sufficient to note that growing up I had a clear sense of my inner voice, which often suggested that I stay behind the scenes so as not to draw too much attention to myself, supporting the necessary inner activity to stay in touch with the formless side of life.

On my seventh birthday, I was reminded how important it was for me to listen to my inner voice on this point rather than challenge the wisdom of it.

I had asked my mother if I could invite some friends over for a party to celebrate my birthday – something I had never requested before because, as mentioned above, I always tried to avoid being a burden to my parents.

The party had all the elements you'd expect: specially invited friends, games, cake, loot bags, and so on. Everything was fine outwardly, but inwardly I found being the center of attention overwhelming, even if only for a few hours.

Fueled by all the special attention, my ego ballooned in size. Unable to channel this energy in a balanced way, I ended up acting like a total imbecile. My best friend at the time was so perturbed by the outer change in my personality that he actually left my party. Before walking out of my house, he gave me a penetrating look and said I was being "fake" and acting like a "totally different person."

The sting of truth struck me at the core of my being. On the surface I knew he was just being a kid, but below the surface, I was equally aware that he was speaking directly from his soul to mine, reminding me of how far I had moved away from the essence of my true self.

During the party I had completely lost touch with the true center of my being. As a result, I became so overly identified

Before the party

with my ego that I ended up acting in a way that was a complete fabrication. It was an important lesson that left a lasting impression.

Not in an emotionally scarred way. Rather, it was a potent reminder to watch for that sort of unchecked ego expansion from happening again, and to keep it in check if it did.

Chapter 3

Connecting to the Formless Dimension

THROUGHOUT MY CHILDHOOD, I knew that the most important thing for me to do was stay connected to the formless dimension. As a result, I often felt like I had one foot in the world of form and one foot in the formless – a kind of nondual citizenship that made me feel like I was always at home wherever I happened to be. And if I ever felt this connection slipping away, I had several ways to bring it back.

I don't know how or when I discovered these methods, but a few of the main ones were watching my reflection in the mirror until my awareness expanded beyond all boundaries, tuning into the subtle energetic or vibratory quality of the phenomenal world, and breathing into my belly until a feeling of absolute fullness filled my entire body.

Even though I was constantly reconnecting with my true nature as a child, I knew that one day I would have to relinquish my enjoyment of it. I can even recall the feeling of absence during those moments when I noticed the loss of this connection. It would suddenly occur to me that something fundamental was missing from my life, as if something significant had been forgotten. But as soon as I noticed this feeling, I would use one of my methods to reconnect.

Among these various methods, the one that I used most often involved an intentional movement or shift of attention away from the outer world of form and into the background of awareness, or what is called *witnessing* by many spiritual teachers and nondual traditions today. Witnessing is a basic quality of the soul, and is often equated with a mirror because it functions in a similar way. It is the part of our being that is always in the background observing what is going on inwardly or outwardly without attachment or aversion.

By deliberately heightening my sense of this mirrorlike awareness, I could evoke the experience of being a witnessing presence. From here, the inner shift needed to reconnect with my true nature was accessible by *tracing back the witness* to its source. The shaded box below explains how to reproduce this shift in your own consciousness.

> **Tracing Back the Witness**
> Find a serene setting outdoors, ideally with a view of the horizon. Pick a point just above the horizon. Next, slightly cross your eyes to engage your peripheral vision. Do not look at anything directly. Just notice everything in your field of vision (people, buildings, trees) without getting distracted by anything in particular. Keep your attention fixed in this manner until your awareness becomes like a mirror. Then allow yourself to sink into the background of this mirrorlike awareness as fully as possible.

For me, the movement always felt like passing through a window that opened up to a boundless field of pure awareness extending indefinitely behind me. Once I allowed myself to open up to the endless expansion located behind my body, a vast presence would emerge that generated the feeling that I was a formless being inhabiting a human form.

As I got older, the span of time between forgetting and then remembering to reconnect with my true nature slowly increased. The feeling of absence would arise, but I would be too wrapped up in the outer play of life to take the time to withdraw from the visible world of form and reconnect with the formless dimension found within.

It was during these times, in particular, that I was reminded that there would come a time, a decisive point on my path in this life, when I would have to deliberately stop connecting with the formless dimension altogether.

Long before that moment came, I had discovered another method to consciously amplify the connection. This technique had the added element of eliciting spiritual truths that I knew were extremely important for me to remember. I discovered this method while looking in the mirror one day. I don't know how old I was when I first started doing this, but I suspect it was around the age of four or five.

Regardless of whenever it began, throughout most of my childhood, I often felt compelled to look at myself in the mirror as a way of deliberately widening my awareness. I would begin this activity by asking myself the perennial self-inquiry question: "Who am I?"

While watching my reflection in the mirror, I would hold this question in my mind until the feeling of being a witnessing presence emerged. Then I would allow myself to merge with this witnessing presence in order to experience it as fully as possible.

The result of intentionally doing this while looking in the mirror caused my awareness to expand beyond the confines of my physical body. Within a fairly short amount of time, I was watching myself engaged in this mirroring exercise from a point of view that was outside and all around my body.

Ordinarily, we assume that our awareness is located inside the body (or the head), but during these *out-of-body* or *beyond-the-body* moments, I knew that this was not so. I saw that our true nature is an expandable field of awareness that surrounds and permeates our physical forms. This is why mystics often say that the soul is not in the body, but rather that the body is in the soul.

Once I reached this wider perspective, I'd let my awareness spread out even further, drifting away from my body in all directions. Eventually, my being expanded to such a degree that all sense of separation from external reality completely dissolved, and I became one with everything.

This nondual experience was immediately followed by a recognition of the **absolute truth**. I would realize that my existence as a self-aware human being, and the physical world I perceived all around me, are co-emergent emanations of one all-pervading source and substance manifesting as everything in creation.

It was an absolutely thrilling discovery to behold. Yet, no matter how many times I reached this level of spiritual realization, the all-encompassing outlook of this perspective was too overwhelming. The absolute fullness and clarity of nondual perception was so extraordinary that I had a hard time accepting that this was the true nature of reality. As a result, I would pull away from it and let my awareness shrink back inside my body.

Still, in spite of my inability to sustain this revelation of the oneness of everything, I felt compelled to replicate these nondual moments throughout childhood. And even though I wasn't able to embody nondual awareness in any permanent way, soon after recoiling, another **epiphany** would flood my consciousness.

It would occur to me that the real *me*, or my true nature as a formless being, had a tendency to fall asleep in the denser substance of physical reality. This insight would then remind me once again that this world is constantly flowing into and out of existence from the same formless source that gave rise to my own awareness.

I performed this mirror gazing exercise throughout my childhood. I even learned to accelerate the process by contemplating the idea that I was more than my body, and that the image of my face was not my real face.

Every time I performed this exercise, it elicited the same altered states of awareness I just described, and in the most rarified moments, opened my whole being up to the absolute truth. How to trigger the same awakening in your own being is explained in the shaded box below.

> **Mirror Gazing**
> Sit or stand in front of a large or full-length mirror. Look directly into one of your reflected eyes with a steady gaze. Avoid blinking. If your attention drifts, gently bring it back by focusing on the pupil of your chosen eye in the mirror. Once your attention is unwavering, repeat the following affirmation inwardly as you gaze at your reflection: *I have a face but I'm not only my face.* Then ask yourself: *Who am I?*

It can feel quite weird to experience your awareness separating from your body and becoming a detached observer, especially while staring at yourself in a mirror. Even stranger, seeing other faces as well as having your own face change in appearance often happens while mirror gazing. Some faces you'll recognize, others you won't. Even faces from a past life can come through. All these faces are actually aspects of yourself you're not fully aware of. Just keep watching in an open and relaxed way. As long as you're willing to accept the truth about yourself, you'll eventually process and integrate the subconscious material behind these projections while simultaneously liberating your original face.

I discovered another spiritual skill during my childhood, which was based on perceiving the energetic basis of reality. It was like having access to a metaphysical channel that televised the mystical process throbbing at the heart of creation, and I could tune in and watch any time. The technique to do so involved heightening my vision by staring intently on seeing the energetic quality of air.

I would focus my inner eye outwardly through my actual eyes in such a way that my outer vision grew increasingly acute, eventually becoming so sensitive that I could discern that first the air, and then everything else in my visual field, was made up of billions of energetic particles continuously flashing into and out of existence.

As long as I stayed with this rarefied perception, objective reality would become increasingly pixelated until everything dissolved into an energetic field of vibrating prismatic points of light. This subtle perception would then deepen, initially revealing that everything is made of the golden light of creation, followed by the deepest realm of reality knowable – the unmanifested blackness of the formless dimension.

Shortly after reaching the limits of this sublime mode of knowing, the process would reveal the same perceptions in reverse order. The golden light would re-emerge out of the dazzling darkness of the formless dimension, followed by the granulated energy field, and then the ordinary perception of the phenomenal world.

As with my mirror gazing exercise, I would awaken the absolute truth using this method, which also led to another epiphany. I would realize that the reason most people fail to appreciate the true nature of reality is because we normally only see the physical side of reality. In the absence of perceiving the underlying formless dimension of life, the understanding that reality is a nondual union of form and formlessness is usually forgotten.

For added context, this extrasensory mode of perception is not without its references in the spiritual literature of the world. According to C.W. Leadbeater, a prominent member of the **Theosophical Society**, it is possible for a person to develop microscopic vision by extending an etheric tube from

the third eye. In addition, Stephen Phillips, another Theoso-
phist, claimed that the third eye's microscopic vision is capable of observing objects as small as quarks.[1] The shaded box
below contains an exercise designed to cultivate the ability to
perceive the energetic layers underlying the material world.

Quantum Gazing
Take a minute to clear your mind with your eyes closed.
When you're ready, open your eyes and spend a few moments gazing steadily at a fixed point in space. Then expand your view and remain aware of everything without
focusing on anything in particular. Next, intend to see everything in its quantum reality. As an aid, affirm that your
awareness is arising from the same underlying energetic
source manifesting physical reality. Then wait while watching for fleeting points of light. Eventually, reality will appear rasterized or pointillistic. Once it does, maintain this
rarefied perception until the deeper luminous and nirvanic
dimensions reveal themselves.

Another activity that kept me connected to the formless
dimension occurred during a recurring dream I had as a child.
It would be more accurate to refer to these dreams as **astral
projections**, but at the time I didn't think of them this way. I
only knew that they were far more exciting and tactile than
any other dreams.

They always started the same way. I would find myself
outside my house in the twilight hours of night. Right away,
I'd realize what was happening and start levitating with my
astral or *dream body*, flapping my arms like wings to assist in
the ascension. Once I was capable of flight, I would turn my
attention upwards, eager to travel beyond the outermost edge
of existence.

Like a rocket blasting into outer space, I'd soar high into
the night sky, beyond the clouds and even the stars, watch-

ing joyfully as everything disappeared in the distance below. Seconds later, I was in a totally transcendent place, an endless realm of starless space. My astral body dropped. Only awareness remained. I would pause here for a while, enjoying the sensation of dwelling in this higher realm of formless being.

Then, when I felt ready, I'd dive back towards the Earth, regain my astral body during re-entry, and continue flying around my neighborhood, exulting in the thrill of flight. I'd glide swiftly over the rooftops of all the townhouses in the complex where I lived as a child, often swooping down and whipping through the labyrinthian maze of narrow streets and pathways, before returning to my bed.

There was one more enlightening activity that I repeated throughout my childhood, which left a particularly deep and lasting impression on me.

Each summer, while vacationing at our usual spot up at Albion Hills, I would sit by the campfire at night and let the blistering heat melt the layers of my personal identity away. Body, mind, memories, emotions, and thoughts all peeled off like shedding skin, slowly revealing the underlying presence of nondual being.

Once I was resting in this original state of being, I'd continue gazing into the hearth while pondering the true meaning and purpose of life. Invariably, my musings would take me back to a distant period where I envisioned the dawning of human awareness.

I would picture our primordial ancestors also sitting by a fire contemplatively, periodically staring up at the stars in awe of the mystery of existence. Then I would deepen this act of fire gazing, concentrating on the core of the fire even more intently. Eventually, glowing pieces of ember would become unstable and fall over. As they did, I'd visualize the creation and destruction of human societies over vast epochs of time.

I would imagine humans evolving together, starting with tribal societies, growing into more complex cities and states, flowering into the great civilizations of the past, until culminating in the present era of our modern world.

This act of fire gazing, coupled with superimposing the evolutionary journey of humanity from the distant past to the present, would evoke a powerful epiphany. I would get the distinct impression that the real purpose behind humanity's continuous societal advancement was not to establish bigger, more sophisticated civilizations.

Rather, it would dawn on me that all this material progress is part of a deeper process that is providing the necessary conditions for humanity to continue evolving into higher states of consciousness, until a collective state of enlightened awareness is reached.

And, along with this sweeping vision of the divine destiny of the human race, I would remember that the purpose of my own life was to help advance this endeavor by staying awake to my true nature in order to share this primordial dimension of being with others one day.

Looking back now as I write this, it seems strange that, as a kid, I knew how to transform my consciousness in all these different ways without any prior knowledge or instructions. And yet somehow I did. I know this wisdom came from my soul and not my mind. But how did it get there? I can only surmise that it was carried over from my former lives because I'm fairly certain that I've awakened and been a **guru** during previous incarnations.

Chapter 4

The Temptation of Power & Confronting Evil

THROUGHOUT MY CHILDHOOD I was capable of interpreting most of my dreams. I would often wake up in the middle of them knowing what they meant. If I couldn't figure out what a particular dream meant in the middle of the night, I would go back to sleep knowing that I could easily recall it in the morning, and at that point, just before opening my eyes, I was usually able to grasp their meaning. However, there was one anomaly that kept recurring throughout my childhood that was not so easy to discern or deal with.

Every so often I was visited by an occult being, which, as a kid, I figured was the devil. He would appear as the Count, a vampire puppet from the TV show *Sesame Street*. I know how crazy this sounds, but at the time I was aware enough to know the difference between fantasy and paranormal activity.

I recall intuitively knowing that this being had the ability to change his appearance at will, and that he had chosen this particular form to appeal to my childlike sensibility in as disarming a way as possible. At the same time, it was clear to me that this entity was compelled by some supernatural law to appear in a way that was a more accurate reflection of his sinister and duplicitous nature.

I was no older than five or six when these encounters began. I was aware that secular society had rejected the existence of metaphysical beings, whether demonic or angelic. On a deeper level, however, I knew that this being was very real and came from an unseen dimension beyond the physical.

On the night of each visit, the devil would first approach me in the dream state and telepathically prompt me to open my eyes so that we could continue communicating, albeit nonverbally, in the waking state.

The devil always had one purpose in mind: to try and convince me to follow him. In exchange for my subservience, he offered to grant me supernatural abilities not usually accessible to people in the ordinary world.

He was also capable of reading my mind and knowing my inner thoughts. I knew this because his offer spoke directly to a childhood interest I had in acquiring paranormal powers, or what the Hindus call *siddhis*. But even from a young age, I knew that the only correct way to acquire these abilities was through the grace of God.

Once in a while, though, the thought would occur to me to accept the devil's offer, reasoning that the powers he held out could be used to help others, and that my motivation to do so would cancel out any negative consequences. But once again, I had enough understanding of spiritual matters to realize that this was a self-deceptive trap. Deep within, I knew that the devil would take more than was given, and that, in the end, I would lose everything and gain nothing.

I never mentioned these encounters to anyone, including my parents. Like most people, I knew they wouldn't know how to handle the situation. They'd either discount the reality of what was going on, or avoid talking about it out of discomfort. And even if I could have convinced my parents that these occult encounters were real and not a sign of mental illness, I didn't think there was anything they could do to help me other than try to convince me that the whole ordeal was nothing more than a series of bad dreams.

During this same period of my life, I was visited by other seemingly more benevolent entities. Before falling asleep, I'd sometimes see otherworldly creatures flying into this physical realm through a portal that appeared out of thin air, far off in the distance outside my bedroom window.

These creatures had the heads and bodies of hairless monkeys and the taloned wings and feet of bats. They were extremely thin with translucent copper toned skin, making the bones of their skeletons visible. There were usually two or three of them perched outside my bedroom window, hanging upside down from the eavestrough. They never tried to communicate with me, although they often giggled and whispered to each other to pass the time, while seemingly keeping an eye on me.

I had seen similar looking creatures made of stone on top of cathedrals and buildings before, but at the time, I had no idea that they were called gargoyles, nor that according to medieval religious beliefs, their grotesque form was intended to scare evil spirits away. All I knew for sure was that the beings outside my window were not statues.

While a part of me was mildly comforted by the notion that these supernatural creatures may have been looking out for me, I was never completely sure if they were there to protect me, or if they were in allegiance with the devil, watching me like jail guards to make sure I didn't go anywhere. At the time, I was only certain that their presence coincided with visitations from the devil.

On the night of every encounter, the devil would demonstrate his telekinetic powers by switching the lights on in my bedroom, forcing me to open my eyes. And there, under the incandescent light illuminating waking reality, I would see him standing beside my bed, intuitively knowing that he had materialized out of some unseen dimension beyond the physical, returning to tempt me with the promise of paranormal powers.

I often wondered how the devil was able to get by the gargoyles undetected if they were, in fact, there to protect me.

On a few occasions I even looked peripherally to see if the gargoyles were watching over me, but they were always asleep when the devil was present. One time I mustered up enough courage to turn my head sideways to see if I could wake them up somehow, but the devil immediately sensed my intention and forced me to leave them alone using mind control, which rendered me unable to think or move.

Although I had no power to stop these visitations from occurring, there was an enjoyable aspect to engaging in telepathic conversations with the devil. We would discuss mysterious things, exploring topics and ideas that no one else did in the ordinary world. He had the ability to open my mind to profound levels of occult knowledge that I never would have been able to access or otherwise comprehend.

At the same time, my mind was incapable of retaining any of this information. Everything the devil shared with me would slip away as soon as the meaning was understood, and implied in this strange erasing effect was an unspoken expectation that I would have to follow him if I wanted to retain the vast knowledge he possessed. I always knew that this was a deceptive offer, and that the price for acquiring his knowledge would not be worth the cost of whatever he wanted in exchange.

There was another offer that the devil held out in order to persuade me to follow him. It was a temptation he knew I found particularly difficult to resist: the promise of flight. After unsuccessfully tempting me with the promise of paranormal powers, the devil would sometimes appeal to my flying dreams as a way to coax me out of bed in order to follow him. He would say things like, "I can teach you how to fly with your physical body, and reveal many other wonders beyond this world. You just have to follow me."

I was always apprehensive. I had no control over being visited by the devil. However, when it came to accepting his offers, it was always clear to me that I had a choice in the matter. In fact, my choice was paramount.

These encounters probably went on for about a year. Yet, in spite of the devil's numerous attempts to persuade me, only once did I agree to go with him: the night I decided to tentatively accept his promise of physical flight. I remember feeling older and a bit more daring at the time, so I decided to see if the devil could really show me how to fly in the physical realm.

On the night it happened, the devil led me to the landing at the top of the stairs outside my bedroom. Then he instructed me to stand perfectly still. Next, using occult powers, he released me from the force of gravity. Incredibly, I began levitating, slowly rising into the air, higher and higher. Within seconds, I was hovering about six feet high.

The thrill of levitating was terribly exciting. An ecstatic rush of euphoria filled my small body. Sensing my elation, the devil began telepathically speaking to me with a kind of gleeful enthusiasm. "You see?" he exclaimed excitedly. "You see how easy it is? And I can show you a lot more!"

But as soon as I heard those words, I knew that I'd made a terrible mistake. I had gone too far by accepting the devil's offer. To redeem myself, I knew I had to reject this deceptive entity and everything it represented.

Right away the devil sensed the firmness of my resolve to turn away from him and immediately released me. I fell fast and hit the ground hard.

As I approached the two stairs I ended up landing on, I was struck by the fear that I might fall down the rest of the stairwell and hurt myself. Luckily, I found my balance before that happened. But I still hit the ground with so much force that the impact sent a shocking jolt through my body.

I landed with such a loud thud that my immediate concern was that the noise would arouse my parents from their sleep. I was horrified by the thought that they might witness this unsanctified and paranormal activity.

Thankfully, they didn't awaken. Even if they had, however, it's unlikely that they would have seen this occult visitor. Although the devil was standing in the middle of the hallway when this event transpired, he dematerialized soon after releasing me from his occult clutch.

That moment marked the end of this ordeal, although another terrifying event followed a few years later.

When I was eight years old, I was almost kidnapped after school one day. A black van pulled up beside me just as I was about to cross the street on my way home. There were two men inside the van, and the one on the passenger side opened his door and tried to lure me inside.

Incredibly, earlier that same day, an assembly had been held in the school gymnasium that prepared me for this exact sort of situation. Three visiting police officers gave a presentation on what to do if approached by strangers trying to abduct us. They detailed some of the tactics kidnappers use to trick children into thinking they are trustworthy, including what they might say to lure you inside their vehicle.

Almost word for word, the man in the van said what one of the police officers warned us a child abductor might say. My body froze as soon as I realized that these men wanted to kidnap me.

My immediate instinct was to run to the other side of the street, but my body wouldn't budge. I tried to scream "fire," which were the instructions given by one of the officers, but my vocal chords were equally blocked off from my will to do anything physically.

Then suddenly, like a dam finally bursting after a build-up of immense pressure, a powerful force welled up from inside of me and I erupted into action. I ran behind the van and crossed the street without even looking.

I was running as fast as I could, yet everything was moving in slow motion, including me. The air felt as thick as fluid, and every step required as much strength as if I had actually been running underwater.

In real time, it couldn't have taken me more than a minute to make it to my house, but by the time I finally reached the safety of my front door, it felt like I had been running for at least half an hour.

I ran inside and slammed the door shut behind me. Then I went into the kitchen and crept along the wall, making my way towards the closest window in the house that faced the path I had just come running from. I cautiously peered through a crack in the curtains so as not to be seen, ensuring the men from the black van hadn't followed me home.

It must have taken a good ten minutes before I was able to calm down enough to reflect on the serendipity of the assembly held in the school gymnasium earlier that day, certain that the timing of it was an act of divine intervention.

After spending the last few years reflecting on both these ordeals, I now understand why I had to endure them at such an early age.

Regarding the near abduction by kidnappers, this experience impinged upon my soul the understanding that there are real forces of evil operating in the world, which is something I never would have understood or appreciated as fully had I not experienced it in such a direct way. Added to this is that when evildoers are plotting to harm us, God is just as active implementing a plan to protect us.

Regarding my ordeal with the devil, I learned that human beings have free will on the spiritual path and can choose to follow divine guidance or reject it and go astray. By making the right choice in this situation, I also gained the confidence of knowing that I could probably identify and avoid other potential pitfalls on the path.

In addition, defeating the devil helped remove the self-centered aspect of my desire to acquire paranormal powers, which allowed some of these same abilities to unfold safely over the ensuing years. The most notable being the ability to channel spiritual light. But more on that in the final chapter.

Before concluding this chapter, I want to point out that I wasn't going to include this story in the final version of this book because of the modern tendency to reduce these kinds of experiences to metaphor and psychology only. But I know that my fight with the devil was with an actual occult being who materialized into the physical world from a subtler dimension of reality.

Regardless of whether that explanation is fashionable in today's world, one thing is certain. Encounters with a devil-like being have been reported by mystics throughout history as a meaningful stage on the spiritual path. Two of the most famous examples are Jesus resisting the seductions of Satan while fasting in the desert and Buddha defying Mara while sitting in meditation under a tree.

Figuratively speaking, such stories clearly illustrate that we all have to overcome evil temptations in life. But these accounts also reveal that confrontations with metaphysical beings who embody corruptive and challenging forces can and *literally* do occur in the lives of mystics.

Chapter 5

The Discovery of an Unbreakable Connection

I GREW UP IN a religion-free zone. Although my parents were baptized as Christians, as adults they renounced their adherence to organized religion. As a result, I wasn't exposed to any particular religious or dogmatic beliefs during most of my childhood. When I was around seven years old, however, a spiritual teacher moved into our neighborhood who quickly became a trusted member of the community.

His name was Mr. Michael, and he and his family made their presence known shortly after moving in. They started spreading the message that they were holding Bible meetings in their house, essentially opening up their home to any of the kids in the neighborhood who wanted to learn about the teachings of Jesus.

I was very skeptical about attending. This was during the 1980s when televangelism exploded in popularity and many well-known televangelists were being exposed as charlatans and embezzlers.

I remember the first meeting vividly. Feelings of apprehension stirred about inside me while waiting outside. But as soon as Mr. Michael's wife opened the door to their home, all my worries melted away. She had the sweet **aura** of a loving mother, and true to her matronly energy, warmly invited us all in.

My first impression was that they hadn't fully moved in yet. With few worldly possessions, they owned very little furniture beyond the essentials, and the walls were quite bare. I once asked Mr. Michael about this, and he said they chose to live humbly as their way of following the teachings of Jesus. They also didn't own a TV, but they did have one luxury item nobody else I knew had: an upright wooden piano.

That first Friday night we all sat on the living room floor of their sparsely furnished home wondering what to expect. A long couch sat invitingly against the back wall, but it was off limits to prevent arguments over who got to sit on it.

Mr. Michael eventually came downstairs carrying a large tan guitar. He emanated love and peace, and similar to the impression created by his wife's welcoming presence, any lingering doubts quickly dissipated in the disarming field of his comforting aura.

He had striking blue eyes, and a long, narrow face that looked even longer because of his full-length beard. He wore workmen's clothing, much like my own father did, and I remember wanting to know what kind of work he did.

Mr. Michael introduced himself and his wife, followed by their three children, and then proceeded to confess his faith as part of his introduction: "We are simple Christians who are inspired by the love and sacrifice of Jesus."

I was deeply affected by the sincerity and modesty with which Mr. Michael proclaimed his love for Jesus. Here was a man, I thought to myself at the time, who had found an enduring sense of love in his heart through his devotional faith in Jesus, and was so moved by what he felt that he was inspired to share his discovery with others so that they might find it, too.

Mr. Michael went on to explain that the Good News Club was a place where we could come together and sing and dance and pray as a way to invite the love of Jesus into our hearts. Before starting the activities of our first meeting, Mr. Michael asked us if we had any questions.

"What kind of work do you do?" I asked, eager to get an answer to the one question on my mind.

"I am a carpenter just like Jesus," he replied.

Once again, I was deeply moved by his candor. It was clear from the way he answered that he admired Jesus so much that he had modeled his entire way of life after him. And that is how it began.

Over the course of the next year and a half or so, I went to the Good News Club every Friday night unless something prevented me from being there. And in that humble, sparsely decorated living room, we spent many nights together, singing and laughing while learning about the life of Jesus, the healer and miracle worker who was crucified for sharing his teachings of spiritual salvation over two thousand years ago.

Mr. Michael taught us stories from both the Old and New Testaments of the Bible, especially those concerning Jesus and the miracles that he had performed. His passion brought these stories to life for us. Some of the more popular ones I'd heard from friends or watched in movies on TV, but for the most part, these accounts based on the Christian Gospels were all new to me.

At the time, I wasn't quite sure what to make of the life of Jesus. I often wondered if he had ever actually lived. The story of an immaculate conception was totally unbelievable. Still, I reasoned that it was possible that a man named Jesus was born and lived and taught centuries ago, but that over time, church leaders and believers had embellished and distorted the truth, creating a predominantly fictional character that made Jesus sound like the greatest spiritual hero ever.

Another Christian belief that I had a hard time accepting was the promise of eternal salvation in the afterlife. This belief seemed like an unnecessary substitute for knowing and experiencing the freedom of nondual being so clearly available to anyone in this lifetime. Before meeting Mr. Michael, I had discovered how to experience this boundless dimension inwardly anywhere, anytime. As a result, I never became a follower of Christianity.

To his credit, however, Mr. Michael often espoused that the real power of Christianity wasn't found in any church or belief in the afterlife. According to him, developing a personal relationship with Jesus was the most immediate and lasting source of spiritual salvation in this lifetime.

Although I never felt the need to go through Jesus to access the timeless essence of the soul, I respected Mr. Michael and the passion he had for his ministry. In fact, I sympathized with his mission so much that if the other kids in attendance were ever disrespectful during one of his talks, I would give them a glowering look that said, "Smarten up! This man invited you into his home and is here out of the generosity of his heart. Show some respect." I always felt a certain amount of responsibility to ensure that everyone respected what Mr. Michael was doing.

At the same time, I didn't need to control the situation outright because Mr. Michael was so unconditionally loving that even if the kids in attendance got out of hand (and admittedly I got carried away once in a while myself), he would discipline us in such a caring, direct, and honest manner that we'd immediately calm down and give him our full, loving attention.

In addition to being a kind disciplinarian and a wonderful storyteller, Mr. Michael was also an enthusiastic singer. The guitar was his preferred instrument of choice, but during particularly inspirational evenings he would play the piano for us, too.

He taught us dozens of songs to sing as a group, many of which I still remember to this day. He had a way of getting everyone singing joyfully and freely. It was one of the few places that I felt so personally at ease that I would let myself go completely. I openly shared in the joy of celebrating in song with others and often sang without inhibition.

One of the songs Mr. Michael taught us had a particularly profound effect on me, and still holds a special place in my heart. The lyrics of the song are as follows:

> *God's love is like a circle, a circle big and round*
> *For when you see a circle, no ending can be found*
> *And so the love of Jesus goes on eternally*
> *Forever and forever, I know that He loves me*

This was not one of the more popular songs, but it was my personal favorite. Not because of the words, though. I actually found it difficult to connect with the intended meaning of the song. By stretching my mind a little, I could make the first two lines more personally relevant because they reminded me of the boundless nature of nondual being. The last two lines held less allure. Regardless, the meaning of the words weren't as important as the vibrations that were created by singing the vocals repeatedly.

The song was pitched in a low range, with a slow tempo and a rhythmic quality similar to the chanting of a **mantra**. We would sing this song over and over again, repeating the verses dozens of times, our minds hypnotically whirling like the eternal circle of love we sang about. As I chanted along, my consciousness would slowly spiral into a trancelike state of bliss that sometimes lasted for hours.

A little less than two years after Mr. Michael and the Good News Club magically appeared, it suddenly and sadly disappeared. One evening, Mr. Michael announced that he and his family were moving away in a matter of weeks, and that the meetings would be coming to an end.

Mr. Michael was not a proselytizer, nor did he require us to do anything other than listen and participate. He routinely presented the Good News Club as a place to sing and dance and pray together as a way of inviting the love of Jesus into our hearts, which he explained was something we could do anywhere, anytime.

It was an open invitation each Friday night that was good for the rest of our lives. "No matter where you are or what you are doing," he would often say, "you can always begin to know and feel the Kingdom of Heaven within by opening your hearts to Jesus."

But during the last few meetings we spent together, Mr. Michael became impassioned about making a more permanent vow in order to be saved. He urged us to consider making a lifelong commitment to Jesus as a way to ensure the eternal salvation of our souls.

He even gave us some words we could use to help us do it. He told us to find a quiet place, close our eyes, and pray this simple prayer:

> *Jesus, I ask you to be my Lord and Savior. Come into my heart and wash away my sins.*

He told us that if we prayed using those simple words, Jesus would come and live in our hearts forever.

Again, I was not inclined to believe in the idea of a personal savior, nor did I feel the need for any intermediary to connect with God. My own life had already revealed that God was just a word that referred to the immediacy of knowing and feeling connected to the formless dimension, which anyone could find by going deep within.

As for my sins, I never quite understood what needed to be washed away. I always knew that we are dualistic beings by nature and often have to learn how to do the right things by occasionally experiencing the wrong things.

Beyond the more conventional understanding of learning from our mistakes, if the word *sin* meant anything else to me back then, I thought it more accurately referred to the fear of entering the formless depths of one's being to discover God's presence within. Yet, I truly loved and respected Mr. Michael and wanted to honor him for all he had done, so I accepted his invitation.

On the evening of the last meeting, I left ahead of everyone else. I walked to the end of a laneway and hid behind a fence so that none of the other kids could see me.

It was a cool night and the sky was cloudless. I looked up in awe of the expansiveness of space and all the stars. Such distant jewels of creation, so many other worlds.

Mr. Michael

My metaphysical musings soon gave way to the familiar feeling of formless presence that always revealed itself as the source of everything in existence. I bowed my head and prepared to pray the words given to me by Mr. Michael. But to my surprise, the words I expressed inwardly were not his. I found myself praying to God for something entirely different:

> *God, I know I'm going to forget about You one day. With all my heart, I don't want that to happen. Take my life now so that I can be with You. I don't want to live a life where I can't feel Your Boundless Presence inside me anymore. Let me die now so that I can be*

with You forever. Please take me now. Take my life.
Let me die so that I can return to You now and be
with You forever.

I opened my eyes and was amazed, not only by the words that came out of my heart and mind, but more so by the deep conviction from which they arose. The feeling of wanting to die right then and there was so intense that if God had actually answered my request, I wouldn't have hesitated.

I was absolutely ready to leave this world behind. All the energy connected with my will to live, right down to the very cells of my body, cried out for release. I didn't want to spend another second in my little body being a part of this tiny life.

I knew that I would have been deeply missed by my family and friends and that my death would have been an especially profound source of sadness for my parents. Yet, in that moment, my desire to return to the indivisible mystery at the heart of existence was infinitely more appealing than remaining embodied in this world of form.

My request to leave this world behind went unanswered, but the experience gave me the courage to face my destiny more fully than ever before. More specifically, I always knew that one day I would have to willingly disconnect from the formless dimension, a prospect that always made me feel a little apprehensive. However, as a result of praying to be released from my life on this night, I knew that no matter how much time might have to pass after that connection was broken, my spiritual aspiration would eventually lead me back to God. In other words, my true nature would always remain at the core of my being waiting for rediscovery.

Chapter 6

Disconnecting from the Formless Dimension

I SEVERED MY CONNECTION from the formless dimension approximately three years later. I always knew that this moment would come and that it was something I had to do when the time came.

The method I used to disconnect was based on a simple observation. I saw that most adults breathe from their upper chest, using only the top portion of their lungs, whereas all babies and most children breathe from the belly up, using far more lung capacity.

I was still breathing from the bottom of my belly at this point in my life. I discovered early on that deep breathing in this area produced a profound sense of fullness in the body, and that by moving deeper into this feeling of wholeness, it is possible to merge with the formless dimension of being. It was another method I used to reconnect with my true nature.

By choosing to breathe from the top of my lungs only, I knew that I would eventually lose touch with this nondual core of my being. Inevitably, I would become more identified with my bodily form, while my connection to the formless dimension would gradually diminish, until it was completely forgotten. I even had a clear insight into the reason why I had to go through with this decision.

Deep down I always knew that the ultimate purpose of my life was to help others discover the same awakened state of nondual awareness that I enjoyed. To be an effective guide for others, I had to experience the same loss of true nature as everyone else in order to rediscover it so that I could show others how to regain it, too.

Because of my experience on the last night of the Good News Club, I also knew that I would eventually rediscover my true nature in a permanent way, and, in the process, gain a better understanding of what was necessary to awaken and maintain this level of self-realization.

The moment to accept this new direction came one day at the age of eleven. I was in the upstairs bathroom of my childhood home. I had just performed my mirror gazing exercise and was about to step into the shower when I felt an overwhelming urge that it was time to disconnect from my true nature. It welled up from the formless depths of my being like a shadow eclipsing the clear light of my soul.

Inwardly, I was prepared for this moment. I knew that the time had finally come for me to stop breathing from my belly and start breathing from the top half of my lungs only. Soon after changing my breathing pattern in this way, I also stopped practicing the other exercises I had maintained throughout my childhood.

The results took effect gradually. Over the course of the following year, the amount of time I spent reconnecting with my true nature slowly diminished until it was almost completely forgotten. The only impression that remained was this vague notion that there was this "thing about myself" that I once knew how to connect with that made me feel whole.

During the period of spiritual amnesia that followed, I became an agnostic. My outlook on life became so one-sided and materialistic that I eventually ended up denying the validity of any sort of metaphysical or spiritual reality. All memory of the formless dimension completely receded from my inner life.

At the same time, my adolescence didn't pass without any spiritual experiences. When I first became sexually active, I experienced a powerful rising of **kundalini** energy. An electrifying bolt of energy shot up through my spine and exploded like a ball of lightning inside my head. This brilliant blast of white light burned all thoughts from my mind and left me in a blissful state of emptiness that lasted for hours.

A few days later, another powerful arousal of kundalini energy made me feel twice as large as my bodily form, which left me feeling both physically taller and spiritually higher for several days.

These initial experiences with kundalini energy soon led to the inner discovery and development of **tantra** techniques used in various forms of sexual yoga. By experimenting and following my body's natural sense of intelligence, I learned to manipulate these potent forces to maximize the bliss of sex.

Chapter 7

Other Significant Events During Adolescence

TWO OTHER SIGNIFICANT EVENTS occurred during this same period of my life. The first was discovering the transformative power of writing. I wrote a poem for my first girlfriend soon after we broke up. It was about oneness and the unifying force of love that had bonded us to one another.

Part of the inspiration for writing this poem came from realizing that I was overindulging in sex and using it as a substitute for the more enduring sense of satisfaction that comes from being connected to the formless dimension – something I recalled freely enjoying when I was younger. After composing this poem, I felt a renewed commitment to rediscover that unconditionally joyful state of nondual being.

I still had no idea how to reconnect with my true nature, but I felt that writing, and in particular writing poetry, could help me to access and maybe even restore that lost feeling of wholeness. So, from that moment on, I continued writing as one of my methods of inquiry, cleaving at some understanding of the absolute truth using words.

Most of this writing took the form of short aphorisms and syllogisms. Alongside this kind of writing, I made a personal vow to master the art of poetry, hoping to use this form of literature as a way to explore the mysteries of existence. To support this spiritual activity, I took a creative writing course in night school.

Soon after starting the course, I felt compelled to write a series of short stories summarizing the previous eighteen years of my life. The short story format drew me in because it allowed me to explore specific periods and significant experiences of my life without having to try to weave the meaning of my entire life together.

A prolific period followed. The words flowed easily. Over the course of the school term, I produced several short stories, all drawn from my personal life and history.

My teacher was pleased with the work I was submitting, and one story, in particular, caught his attention. It was inspired by the highs and lows of being in love with someone. Although deeply metaphorical, this story explored the reality of what it was like for me to awaken sexually.

My teacher asked me to explain where the inspiration for the story came from, and more specifically, if it was something I had dreamed up, or if it was based on personal experience.

Slightly uncomfortable with the unwanted attention, and also embarrassed to reveal the truth, I avoided his question. But he persisted.

I finally answered that it came from personal experience. He could tell I wasn't comfortable talking about my writing or myself and didn't persist in inquiring further. He just told me to continue writing in one of those special moments sometimes shared between teacher and student.

We hardly spoke again throughout the remainder of the course, but I took his encouragement to heart. I continued to write and eventually developed an interest in fusing prose and poetry together in an attempt to transform my consciousness.

After the course ended, I tried to write more short stories, but I was unable to produce anything new. Everything I could think of writing was a retelling of the same themes and experiences that I'd already explored in those original stories.

I eventually came to the conclusion that my reason for writing them down had more to do with releasing my personal identity from the story of my past, which it did. After writing those semi-autobiographical stories, I no longer felt the need to dwell on the past in order to define my sense of self.

This marked an important phase in my personal development. It was the first time following my decision to give up my connection to the formless dimension that I returned to living more fully in the present moment. As a result, I began receiving an influx of spiritual insights, the most significant of which was the importance of *selfless service*.

The sense of liberation that came from transcending the identification with my personal history awakened a potent desire for more spiritual freedom. To satisfy this yearning, the wisdom in my soul suggested engaging in selfless service to completely dissolve all selfish motives in order to experience being completely egoless. And, although I wasn't aware of it at the time, I now know that this undertaking helped me earn the merit to experience enlightenment.

My decision to engage in selfless service coincided with another teacher's timely intervention during my final year. I was heading to a class when one of my teachers from my first year approached me in the hallway and asked me if I wanted to become a peer mediator. I hadn't done any extracurricular activities before then, nor had I spoken with this teacher after being a student in his class four years prior. However, as part of my commitment to selfless service, I wrote an inspired letter about the importance of becoming involved in the school community that was printed in the school newspaper a few days earlier.

October 1991 – The B

Seize the Day

"My years in high school were the happiest, most memorable times of my life." This is a statement I have heard parents, teachers, university students, and people from all walks of life proclaim. Now in

Grade 13 at Brebeuf, I find myself questioning what memories of high school will I recall later in life? Writing an article for The B for the first time in five years is a landmark for me.

Recently, I realized how many extracurricular activities are available at Brebeuf (and my lack of involvement in them) when I inquired about becoming a leader for Grade 9 Orientation. The list on the back of the application was intimidating. I was going to list all the groups, activities, and sports that I never got involved in, but it would have exceeded the 250-word limit for this article. Suffice it to say, the purpose of this article is to leave a brief message to any students who, like me, just show up for class and then leave school as soon as it's over. Simply and briefly, here it is:

Participating in extracurricular activities is not only an important source of enjoyment at school, it seems to be a key factor in creating lasting memories that you can enjoy later on in life. So take advantage of all Brebeuf has to offer and seize the opportunity to make your landmark in the universal memories of high school.

The publication of this article, combined with the serendipity of my teacher's invitation to become a peer mediator and my newly acquired motivation to volunteer, all came together at just the right time. I knew it was something I had to do, so I accepted on the spot.

I immediately saw the value of learning about the process of mediation, an activity in which a neutral third party – the mediator – assists two or more parties in resolving a dispute.

A basic tenet of mediation is to reach a solution that both parties can agree on, and if possible, help transform the antagonistic nature of their relationship in the process.

Not only was I grateful for the opportunity to help others resolve their disputes, I felt this training was more valuable than anything else I'd ever learned in school, providing conflict resolution and communication skills that I never would have learned so easily or as quickly from the school of hard knocks.

By the time I graduated from high school, the importance of selfless service, combined with my desire for personal and spiritual growth, had become the primary focus of my life. So, I decided to dedicate a year to both.

I had been admitted to York University for a general arts degree in English, but I deferred my acceptance until the following year so that I could focus on exploring the possibility of self-transcendence through selfless service and other means.

My father was unsupportive of my decision to go to university to get a Bachelor of Arts degree, and I knew that he would be even less supportive of my decision to take a year off. He wanted me to enroll in a business program or at the very least get a Bachelor of Science degree, which he felt was a more pragmatic and wiser career move. Fortunately, I figured out how to deal with this dilemma.

I informed my father that I had no interest in going to university to become more employable. He then asked me to explain my reasoning for wanting to get a university education, to which I replied that I only knew that I was searching for the meaning of life. I knew he would refuse to support my decision based on that answer, which he did, and added that I had to switch programs or he wouldn't give me his blessing.

As anticipated, this led to a stalemate.

Several weeks after the new school term began, my father noticed that I was hanging around the house a lot. When he asked me why I wasn't attending any classes, I informed him that I was unwilling to go to university without his support. Upon hearing this, he was forced to concede, knowing that it was better for me to get a Bachelor of Arts degree than ending up with no degree at all. And best of all, I was free to dedicate an entire year to exploring my spiritual pursuits without my father's interference.

Chapter 8

Entheogenic Explorations

DURING THIS YEAR OFF, I worked as a waiter at Swiss Chalet, a restaurant I had been employed at throughout high school. I used my time at work to continue practicing selfless service, performing as many acts of kindness as possible for my fellow employees. I would serve them coffee on their breaks, cover their shifts if they needed me to, help clear their tables without being asked, bring out their orders for them if they were busy, even lend my car out. Whatever was needed. If there was an opportunity to help someone, I did. No questions asked. No expectations for the favor to be returned.

During my spare time, I also experimented with certain *entheogenic* (God within) or psychoactive substances used by spiritual aspirants for thousands of years. More specifically, I made use of marijuana and hashish, and on a few separate occasions, LSD and psilocybin mushrooms.

I occasionally smoked marijuana with my friends during our last two years of high school. My friends were mainly interested in using it for recreational purposes, but I knew that if used with a more spiritual purpose and intent, marijuana and other entheogens could be potential catalysts for accessing mystical states of awareness. So, I'd often turn my attention inwards, or physically separate myself from the group and wander off alone in order to explore the mind expanding effects of marijuana.

My intent for using marijuana was to access any mystical states the drug might produce, while simultaneously observing the subtle shifts that occurred in my consciousness to see if it was possible to duplicate the same effects without using this psychoactive substance.

One night, my friend Jackson dropped by my house and asked me if I wanted to try LSD with him and another friend of ours. He knew I was interested in partaking of this particular substance. Needless to say, I accepted his offer.

Since it was my first time, I was mildly concerned about the side effects of LSD. I had heard the fear mongering about the possibility of suffering from flashbacks years later or irreparably damaging one's brain or DNA.

At the same time, I knew that LSD was clinically proven to be a known catalyst for intense spiritual experiences and that the active compound in LSD was a synthetic drug that produced psychoactive effects similar to *psilocybin* – the active ingredient in the fungus colloquially called *magic mushrooms*, which has been used safely as a sacramental substance in the spiritual and religious ceremonies of different cultures around the world for thousands of years.

Aware of the contemporary wisdom stressing the importance of *set and setting* to ensure a good trip, my mindset was positive. Shortly after ingestion, I suggested going to a park so that we could sit back and observe the effects of LSD as we experienced them. I was mainly attracted to experiencing the oneness of everything reported by many users, but I was also open to experiencing whatever mind altering effects the drug might produce.

On the way to the park, I began noticing some of the initial visual and auditory *echoes* indicating the onset of the drug. The ground began *breathing*, or swelling up and down, and soon after, I saw and heard my first *tracers*: as we crossed the street leading to the park, a streetcar passed by and my attention was momentarily enthralled by the afterimage trails from the bright lights and the reverberating rumble of the heavy rolling metal wheels.

Within minutes of arriving, my companions grew bored and restless. They had both tried LSD before and had more recreational intentions for using it, so as soon as they felt the effects coming on, they wandered off somewhere else.

Once alone, I made my way towards a large metal slide, climbed the narrow ladder to the top and stretched out on the landing. It was late in the evening, somewhere close to midnight. A thin layer of wispy clouds veiled the night sky like a huge translucent canvas, and the city lights, in combination with the moon's natural luminosity, cast a cool, silvery radiance across them.

My intention was to let my mind wander in response to the shape-shifting suggestibility of clouds, while waiting for the molecules of the drug to work their way deeper into my brain. I had no idea that the clouds would become the backdrop for the rapid visionary experience that followed.

Within a short amount of time, the thin, diaphanous layer of cloud cover began to take on darker shades. Soon, distinct images appeared, revealing highly detailed vistas of heavenly and hellish realms that kept morphing into one another in a monochromatic display of shifting Judeo-Christian religious scenes.

One of the scenes that kept reappearing in this nebulous diorama was the Crucifixion of Christ, in which the image of Jesus kept morphing into a whimsical looking form of Satan. A host of angelic beings in the surrounding background also transformed into a retinue of demonic beings in tandem with the transfiguration of Christ and Satan.

Interestingly, I didn't find the iconoclastic imagery of this vision disturbing in the least. In fact, it was mildly humorous. I knew that the stories and symbols of Christianity that I had learned about while growing up and their intended religious significance had only been impinged upon my consciousness in the most superficial way, which is part of what this vision was revealing to me. But on a deeper level, I understood the real message being communicated. If I truly wanted to transform my consciousness and experience the oneness of everything in a permanent way, I had to throw off all forms of dualistic thinking, religious or otherwise.

This revelation ended up being the peak of my first LSD journey. After my friends returned, we made our way home. I told them nothing about my vision. Once home, I spent the remaining hours of twilight lying in bed, letting the lingering effects of the drug wear off before I fell asleep.

During that same year, I took LSD and magic mushrooms a few more times, mainly to compare the effects. I gained some momentary glimpses of the oneness of everything. But, ultimately, the drugs were unfulfilling. After the effects wore off, the question remained: *How can I make the feeling of oneness permanent?*

Chapter 9

Witnessing & Other Strange Stuff

MY DESIRE FOR UNITY CONSCIOUSNESS definitely intensified as a result of my entheogenic explorations and the nondual experiences they elicited. However, the final resolution to my search for enlightenment lay elsewhere.

A pivotal event occurred one day while I was engaged in a philosophical discussion with Jackson and a couple of our friends. We were debating the nature of the self, and at one point in the conversation, the question was posed, "What is it that is going on in our minds that allows us to know that we exist?"

The conversation quickly moved into what is commonly referred to as the Homunculus Argument in consciousness studies. *Homunculus* is a Latin word that means "little man," and the Homunculus Argument is based on the idea that some sort of entity or agent exists inside the head that is ultimately responsible for the subjective awareness that we are thinking, feeling, and perceiving beings.

The problem with positing a homuncular entity or agent is that it still leaves the question of who or what is responsible for the underlying experience of *beingness* itself. To suggest yet another imagined homunculus in order to account for the first entity's experience only creates an infinite regression of smaller and smaller entities ad infinitum – a quandary in consciousness studies referred to as the Homuncular Fallacy.

Our own attempts to resolve this philosophical question moved along the same lines of logic that night, and although we didn't arrive at any satisfactory conclusions, the conversation left a lasting impression on me. It reminded me of this "thing about myself" from my childhood, as well as the mirror gazing activity I often performed back then.

Shortly thereafter, I began doing it again. In addition, as a way to simulate the Homuncular Fallacy, I'd occasionally modify this exercise by adding a second mirror. Standing between two mirrors facing each other at slight angles created a condition of repeating images that allowed me to watch myself looking at myself looking at myself without end.

The infinite self-reference created by this activity became a kind of fractal **mandala** that evolved into an unsolved **koan** that I began contemplating inwardly and constantly: *If I can be aware of myself as a looker, then who or what is the source of this looking?*

The effect generated by holding this question in my mind eventually resulted in the development of a striking split in my consciousness. I became acutely aware of the observing, impersonal aspect of my consciousness, which was something quite distinct from my egoic self.

Occasionally, there were moments when I'd recall having been in touch with this same impersonal state of being during my childhood, but at the time my understanding of witnessing was no longer integrated with the fluency of nondual being I had implicitly known back then. I also didn't know that witnessing is a known stage on the spiritual path.

As a result of this disconnect, I had trouble getting a handle on the emergence of witnessing and the division it created in my consciousness. An example of my confusion is illustrated in a journal entry I wrote during this period:

January 4, 1996

I have been depressed for over a month now. Sometimes a good strong social connection breaks through, but I quickly fall back into despair. Emptiness is my constant preoccupation. My experience of the world is somehow incomplete. I spend so much time trapped inside myself that I miss out on daily conversations, only to realize that I have been staring coldly, emptily into space.

Neither my lack of understanding the stages of awakening, nor the process of dissociating from reality, interrupted the increase in witnessing. Subjectively, it felt like my identity was dividing into two parts: an impersonal side on the one hand, and my personal sense of self on the other. Along with the development of this inner split, there was a distinct sense that my entire identity was transitioning towards witnessing, and that this shift was unstoppable.

The witnessing of my soul eventually grew so strong that it manifested as a mirrorlike presence in the back of my mind. Afterwards, I no longer needed to look at an external mirror in order to evoke this observing presence. It became a permanent fixture in my consciousness. And, again, in terms of my sense of self at this stage in my journey, I grew increasingly identified with this mirror in the back of my mind.

Shortly after this development, I began having all sorts of new subtle experiences, two of which stand out as the most significant in terms of what led to my awakening.

The first was a perception of the roots of egoic activity that used to appear during my childhood, except now these same structures were piled on top of each other, forming a heap in my psyche.

As part of this same subtle experience, I saw several more of these formations in my subconscious mind, which looked similar to stalactites and stalagmites in a cave. At the time I wasn't aware of this, but I now know that these formations are called *sanskaras* in Hinduism and Buddhism, which refer to karmic patterns accumulated from past experience either in this life or in previous lives.

As I understand it, they contribute to the manifestation of specific lessons one still needs to learn to resolve the karma that creates them. In many cases, the experience of enlightenment can eliminate them from the psyche in order to help restore consciousness to its formless purity, which is necessary for the soul to stabilize the enlightened state of being.

In the noetic mode of knowing that accompanied this perception at the time, I managed to figure out that these tapered formations were made from concretions of memory that had slowly been deposited into my subconscious mind through a layering process that matches newer experiences with older ones, creating the proclivities of my ego and personality. I also gathered that the most recent pile was an accumulation of all the unresolved experiences that had unconsciously piled up in my psyche ever since I gave up my connection to my true nature.

Alongside this perception, the very notion of having a personal self was dissolving during this period of my life, which also manifested as part of this same experience. More than once, I observed these mnemonic deposits being pulverized. It was like an invisible mining operation was breaking up the sanskaras in my subconscious mind in order to prepare the ground of my being for the transformation that was to come.

Initially, I had no foresight regarding what to do about this jumbled mound of stuff sitting in my psyche, nor the reason that older formations just like it were being shaken up inside the cave of my subconscious mind. All I knew for sure was that this subtle perception allowed me to disidentify from my ego even more, assisting the shift towards witnessing, which ultimately led to my awakening and, consequently, the rapid removal of the sanskaras from my subconscious mind.

The other notable subtle experience occurred one night at Albion Hills. I'd spent a weekend there alone to contemplate the meaning of the changes occurring in my consciousness. On the Saturday evening of my retreat, I went for a walk on a nearby beach.

It was a warm and windless summer night. Not even the slightest ripple disturbed the lake, creating the perfect mood to grow more reflective. An inverted image of the trees lining the lake on the glassy surface of the water made me think of Hermes Trimegistus' famous formula, "as above, so below."

No sooner had this thought formed in my mind than the idea seemed to manifest in my immediate surroundings. All of a sudden, incredibly powerful winds started blowing, forcing me to retreat to a lifeguard chair.

With one arm covering my eyes and the other stretched out for more shielding, I leaned into the wind and pressed forward, struggling to find my footing at times. I finally reached the chair, anchored myself to the seat on top, and waited for the raging windstorm to die down.

With the wind roaring in my ears, I looked up in awe of how quickly the weather had changed. In less than a minute the night sky went from being completely clear to being covered by these huge, muscular clouds that were surging so swiftly through the atmosphere it was like watching a time-lapse film. The intensity of the scene was so dramatic it felt as if cosmic forces were engaged in some sort of earthly battle.

Then, as abruptly as the mad blast started, it stopped. The momentum generated by the powerful winds whisked all the clouds away, restoring a panoramic view of the heavens. With my gaze still fixed upon the firmament, I felt even more in awe of the invisible and powerful forces animating the natural world. Then came the most delightful vision of my life.

All the stars in the night sky transformed into subtle gem-like structures that descended directly into my consciousness. It was like a chandelier falling from the ceiling of the universe that squeezed itself into my shutting eyes.

It was so sudden and unexpected. The entire experience transpired in the blink of an eye, *literally*. But in the split of a second that it took for my eyelids to close and then open, time stretched into infinity as the firmament descended in dazzling, bejeweling, blissful slow motion.

Because it happened so slowly, I had time to observe the precise details of every single gem constituting this ornate structure. The number and variety of these falling treasures was astounding. Each one looked like a two-dimensional diagram of a three-dimensional object, and because of this, they appeared empty inside. But it was clear to me that they were actually filled with the same medium of higher consciousness they were descending in. Also, the crystalline edges of each gem had a particular color that made each of these luminous jewels glow with a translucent hue.

I had absolutely no idea what to make of this supernal gift at the time, and it wasn't until quite a few years after my awakening that I discovered the significance and purpose for all these metaphysical jewels of consciousness.

A. H. Almaas, a contemporary spiritual teacher and mystic, is the originator of a path to self-realization known as the Diamond Approach. I believe the phenomenon I experienced on this night is comparable to what Almaas refers to as a manifestation of the Diamond Dimension.

Based on my understanding, this is yet another example of the many different types of vehicles that can emerge on the inner journey home. According to Almaas, these gems can appear one at a time, or they can descend all at once, much like the way they did for me.[2]

In my case, after this cosmic chandelier descended into my consciousness, it remained dormant in the unseen depth of my soul until the night of my awakening. If it had been operating in any way throughout this period, it did so without my knowledge. On the night of my awakening, however, this multifaceted structure re-emerged and facilitated an important part of the transformation I underwent that night.

I will elaborate on how this mystical process unfolded in more detail later on. For now, it is sufficient to note that the gems in this vehicle were responsible for transforming the heap of sanskaric material I described earlier into a higher order of being. More specifically, they deconstructed and restructured my egoic self as part of a process that culminated in my consciousness and identity merging with my higher self.

Chapter 10

Going to University & the Emergence of X

AFTER SPENDING A YEAR dedicated to selfless service and my inner spiritual quest, the time to go to university eventually arrived. I was aware that academic work would impinge on my inquiry, but I reasoned that university could still double as a place for me to continue my search intellectually, and perhaps even offer some insight or context for all the subtle changes that were occurring in my consciousness.

I didn't know if my spiritual inquiry was something that was explored in the academic world. I had arbitrarily chosen English as my major when I applied to university because it was my best subject in high school. It never occurred to me to choose another major in order to broaden the scope of available courses. So, out of the courses I could take as an English student, I tried to piece together a curriculum that I thought might help shed some light on my spiritual search.

One course that looked promising was a Humanities option examining Greek and Biblical traditions. I was interested in discovering what Western Philosophy and its wisdom traditions had to say about the possibility of understanding the absolute truth. I also took Biology, Anthropology, English Literature, and Creative Writing.

It was comforting to learn that the Anthropology course emphasized the importance of self-reflexive awareness (becoming aware of your own awareness), which helped normalize the emergence of witnessing to a certain extent. The Greek and Biblical traditions course also played an important role in my eventual awakening. But it was the Creative Writing course that affected me the most profoundly.

My initial reason for taking this course was to continue my personal writing forays as part of an overall effort to transform my consciousness. The instructor for the course was Canadian poet Christopher Dewdney. I had never heard of him before, but during the first class he introduced himself as an explorer of consciousness, as well as someone who had emerged from the sixties as part of a serious movement to transform human consciousness.

I was intrigued, to say the least. For the first time in my life, I felt like I had finally met someone who might be able to offer some sort of insight into many of the non-ordinary states of consciousness that I had experienced on my journey.

Dewdney is a poet with a scientific mind – a dichotomy I found fascinating. I quickly developed an interest in learning everything I could about this man and what he had discovered, so I began studying all his literary works published to date by that time (1993) – a collection of nine books of poetry and two works of non-fiction.

His two non-fiction books exposed me to all sorts of new ideas about the faculties of perception and the relationship between consciousness and experience, yet it was his poetry that had the most impact on me.

The essence of Dewdney's poetic *oeuvre* is an investigation into the limits of perception as a means of knowing. His poems constantly reveal the impermanence of sense impressions and the illusory nature of the self.

I immersed myself in his work and became so absorbed in his writings that it felt like my consciousness went through some kind of alchemical transmutation in order to receive the transmission communicated through Dewdney's poetry.

Looking back, I can also see that, inwardly and secretly, I had acknowledged Dewdney as my guru and engaged in a practice called *guru yoga*. The practice of guru yoga has many variations, but all forms require visualizing the guru as a way

to invoke his or her consciousness. Although Dewdney isn't a
spiritual teacher or guru, I still
chose him to be this kind of figure for me.

I never told Dewdney of his
influence on me, nor to my knowledge was he ever aware of it. Yet,
his literary work, personal presence, and level of consciousness
were all catalysts that helped me
advance spiritually.

Christopher Dewdney

My "downloading" of Dewdney's ideas and poetry, in
addition to spending time in his company and calling him
to mind when not physically present, all helped accelerate a
process of soul ascension that began prior to meeting him but
was thrust upward after coming into contact with him.

The format of Dewdney's writing class was to submit
work anonymously and have it discussed by fellow students.
Occasionally, if we were lucky, we would receive a comment
or two from our esteemed instructor. My poetic abilities were
just beginning to develop at the time, but I managed to get
Dewdney's feedback twice.

The first time was for a poem I submitted that was inspired by Michelangelo's *Statue of David*. Dewdney focused
on it, praising it, while at the same time pointing out that I
(the unnamed author) had become self-conscious towards the
end of the poem and let the inspiration fall from the sublime
heights that both the poem and poet had attained, which was
true. The poem ended with pigeon excrement splattering on
the face of this beautiful image I had sculpted into form using
words and metaphors drawn from the language of geology.

On another occasion I submitted a poem that explored the theme of the impermanence of the body and the eternity of the soul. The poem was written using a traditional rhyming pattern and meter, as well as equally archaic vocabulary. It was written in the first person, metaphorically equating my body to a wax candle, in which my own arms lit the wick to release my soul from its physical form.

In an unexpected turn of events, Dewdney questioned the metaphysical inspiration behind the poem, revealing his agnostic views to me for the first time. He then went on to express a personal distaste for spiritual themes in poetry like the one I had explored.

It was a crushing blow to my confidence, not as a poet, but as a spiritual seeker. I respected Dewdney as a scholar of consciousness so deeply that his comments made me question the validity of my search to discover the absolute truth. But that didn't stop me. Nothing could have. So I pressed on.

On another occasion, I believe Dewdney secretly introduced one of his own unpublished poems for us to critique, and the effect of reading this poem radically altered my state of consciousness. In fact, this mystical experience led to the discovery of another vehicle of transformation that ended up being vital to my awakening.

I wasn't aware of the mantric power of poetry at the time, but this poem was definitely of a mystical order. It was a short poem of several lines or so, which stood out from all the others submitted thus far, both for its content and form.

It had originally been printed on an old dot-matrix printer and photocopied many times over. The fact that it had been printed on outdated technology with distortions created by copies being reproduced from copies led me to suspect that this was not a submission from another student.

Regardless of whoever authored it, reading this poem had a transcendental effect on my consciousness. I cannot recall the poem in its entirety, but I distinctly remember the one line that created the most impact. It read, "a million plates of the moon," and the image evoked by those six words resonated with such poetic force that it caused a profound shift to occur in my consciousness.

As soon as I read that line, a steady stream of silver light poured into my head from up above. It felt as if some occult power of the moon was being channeled through the poem. The next thing I knew, my consciousness was spiraling out of my body, magnetically drawn upwards along this luminous shaft of light.

As my consciousness beamed upwards, everything in the room disappeared into a void of nothingness below. Once this transcendental effect reached its peak, my being felt as bright and wide as the moon itself, radiating blissfully in some starless sky high above my ordinary state of mind.

In conventional reality, I knew that I was hovering about a foot and a half above my body in the classroom. At the same time, it was clear to me that I was no longer solely in the physical world of form. I was amazed at the pristine clarity of this transcendental state of awareness and by how boundless the dimensions of my being had become.

Although this event transpired very quickly in *real time*, subjectively everything happened in slow motion. As a result, I saw the changes as they occurred in my consciousness.

First, I merged with the mirror in my mind, which was illuminated by the steady stream of moonlike light pouring into my head, and the confluence of these two events propelled my consciousness upwards and into what I now know to be the location of my higher self.

At the time, I had no conceptual framework to understand any of this. I only knew that I was remembering something crucial about my true nature and identity, but it was too vague to fully appreciate or stabilize. Ultimately, something more was needed. What happened next was pivotal.

I remembered the nightly metamorphosis from my childhood. It had been so long since I had experienced those mystical states of being that I had nearly forgotten about them. As I recalled this inner journey in its entirety, I realized that the divine spark was sown like a seed in my childhood consciousness, transforming my being in ways that were necessary at the time.

Next, I realized that the transformations of consciousness that this divine spark once facilitated were no longer available in the same way as before. Never again would I become one with the boundless light or dissolve into oblivion before being released into the freedom of formlessness. Never again would I enjoy the inner trip up and down that expanding vortex of numinous energies, accessing spiritual insights about the interrelated nature of consciousness, reality, and the origins of the cosmos.

Thinking that I'd lost something truly important, I felt a deep vacancy within. What I didn't fully appreciate yet was that this inner process had already achieved what it was designed to do. It left many permanent impressions in my soul as intended, each significant in deeply meaningful ways. Moreover, with the loss of the old, something new was about to be born.

The next moment another subtle form appeared in my consciousness. It had the exact same pearly golden luster as the sphere of light, except, instead of a sunlike orb, this new phenomenon emerged in the form of a luminous X that was glowing and pulsating with an equally seductive brilliance. I was immediately entranced by it.

In the midst of this luminous form appearing, I heard Dewdney's voice in the background. He was asking me what I thought about the poem. I knew that he had already asked a few other students what they thought of it, and although I hadn't registered what anyone else had said specifically, I got the distinct impression that none of the comments offered had satisfied Dewdney sufficiently.

I was still hovering above the classroom in a transcendental state of awareness when I heard his voice calling on me in the room below. My awareness partially returned to conventional reality as I searched for some thoughtful response. The luminous X was still present, too, superimposed over my entire field of vision.

It felt heavy being pulled back down into the denser reality of the phenomenal world, although for the time being, I remained in a quasi-transcendental state, still looking down into the room from overhead.

My vision zeroed in on the black and white page below. I stared blankly at it for a few seconds, not knowing what to say or how to describe the effect that the poem had just had on me. I was concerned that if I revealed too much information I would have sounded mentally unbalanced.

I wanted to speak up, to offer some sort of explanation, but I also knew that any verbal or mental activity would draw my consciousness back down inside my body, separating me from the higher state of being I was still mostly immersed in and wanted to sustain.

I finally managed to utter something about the poem having a strange effect on me that I couldn't quite explain. The next thing I remember is the class moving on, while I remained in this higher plane, totally mystified and wondering what to make of this luminous X. A short time later, my consciousness returned to my body while the X disappeared below the threshold of my awareness, where it seemed to sink into my subconscious mind like another seed.

After the class ended, I wandered around campus aimlessly for hours. Every once in a while, I'd settle down in a quiet spot to contemplate the significance of the bizarre glowing X that I sensed was now buried in the unseen depths of my being. I spent the remainder of the day searching for a possible meaning behind this symbol and the purpose for its emergence.

My initial impression was that this phenomenon might be a warning of some kind, signaling that I was at the precipice of a dangerous inner zone better left unexplored. Based on the occult encounters from my childhood, I was aware that there are deceptive traps that can lead one astray on the spiritual path, and a part of me wondered if I was at risk this way once again. The image of an X certainly made me feel like I was exploring something forbidden. This symbol evoked all sorts of associations that suggested this was so.

For example, X is used for marking a wrong answer on a test, and to have a similar sign glowing across the entire field of my awareness made me feel like I might have been moving in a wrong direction. Other associations added to this fear.

X's are used to mark the hidden spot on a treasure map, which is usually somewhere remote and dangerous. In cartoons, X's are drawn instead of eyes to indicate the death of a character. Similarly, X's are used to denote *delete* or *cancel* in many computer operating systems.

While these last two associations fit with the dissolution or death of the ego typically experienced at the moment of enlightenment, at the time, I had no idea that this is a core feature of the process of spiritual awakening.

With all the unnerving associations floating around in my mind, I was worried that I had opened myself up to something potentially destabilizing. Fortunately, there were other associations that influenced my attitude towards this phenomenon in a positive way.

For example, the visual effect of diffraction spikes radiating from candles and other light sources will often create an X pattern. In mathematics, X's are typically used to represent an unknown quantity, which, to me, was suggestive of solving the riddle of existence I was trying to unravel.

Symbolically, X's also refer to "being at a crossroads" or a significant turning point in one's life, which I deeply resonated with. And lastly, the letter X is used as an abbreviation for Christ, which was comforting to a certain extent, although at the time I thought that this was a secularized form of shorthand without any deeper symbolic or spiritual significance.

Years later, I learned that the English letter X comes from the Greek letter *chi*, which stands for the word *Christos* – the spiritual name given to Jesus by his followers in recognition of his divinity. What is less well known is that this symbol is also a mystical device that Jesus used to access his higher self and God in order to perform the miracles he did during his life and ministry.

However, it was actually a literary device called a *chiasmus*, something I had learned about in the Humanities course on Greek and Biblical traditions I was taking at the time, that convinced me to explore this subtle form with a greater degree of trust and confidence.

Today, chiasmus can refer to any crisscross structure that looks like an X. But as a literary device, it refers to a figure of speech that reverses two or more clauses that are related to each other to make a larger point. A modern example is the saying, "Winners never quit, and quitters never win."

This basic structure can exist in a single sentence as in the above example, but it can also be used in longer, more complex passages, such as those found in the Greek and Hebrew texts of the Bible. When used in this way, this literary device creates chiastic structures, giving the text a very symmetrical and recognizable crisscross pattern.

I was aware of the esoteric belief that the Bible contained hidden symbols, and upon learning about this particular pattern, I felt certain that the Bible was replete with this symbol for reasons beyond literary convention. Its presence spoke to me of a much deeper message encoded in the text. This association, above all the others, gave me the assurance I needed to explore the luminous X further.

In the days and weeks following the initial emergence of this phenomenon, the glowing X would spontaneously reappear, superimposing itself over my entire visual field. It didn't matter what I happened to be doing. Suddenly the X would just appear. And whenever it did, I would meditate on it.

Again, I didn't know about the existence of vehicles of transformation at the time, but on an intuitive level I knew that this phenomenon was something worthy of beholding, which is exactly what I did. I sensed it was something potentially transformative, although I had no way of knowing if its influence was positive. All I knew for sure was that it represented something new and mystical.

I now know that this particular vehicle is an example of what is called a *yantra* or *mandala* in the Hindu and Buddhist traditions, respectively. These are symbolic diagrams that are originally received through mystical revelation by someone spiritually adept enough to access them, which can then be used by others during meditation as an aid in the awakening process. They can also be considered manifestations of *sacred geometry*, an esoteric system based on the knowledge that certain shapes carry transformational powers.

The shape of an X is a recurring feature in many yantras and most mandalas. In Buddhist mandalas especially, the two intersecting lines are typically drawn deliberately, but even if not explicitly shown, they are often implied through various elements in the composition. All that to say, the image on the cover of this book can also be used as a mandala or yantra. The shaded box below provides a basic introduction. If you're interested in experiencing the full power of this symbol, additional resources are available on my website.

> **Christ's Cross**
> Position the yantra so that you can look at it, ideally at the same level as your eyes and a comfortable distance away. Maintain a straight spine and avoid blinking. Breathe in and out slowly until your mind is calm and alert. Next, focus on the *bindu*, the dot at the center of the X, until your attention is unwavering. Then, while remaining focused on this center point, slowly broaden your view until you are gazing solely at the X. After a minute or so, close your eyes and watch the yantra imprinted in your mind's eye, allowing it to gradually guide you from within. Follow it as it slowly fades away and you'll be drawn into the underlying state of formless consciousness – our true nature as pure spirit.

Back to my journey, when this mystical form first emerged in my consciousness, it did so in a totally spontaneous way. To help get a grip on its appearance, I began noticing how ubiquitous this symbol was in conventional reality.

X's are used on traffic signs, painted on roads near crosswalks, branded on consumer products in savvy advertising campaigns, and used as a rating for extreme content in books, films, music, and so on. My own generation was also dubbed Generation X around this time, so the term was extensively bandied about in the media. In a nutshell, during this period of my life, X's were popping up everywhere – both inwardly and outwardly.

Looking back now, I can see how grounding this was. I was moving into deeper and subtler inner spiritual terrain and was uncertain where it would lead. Without any sort of map of consciousness or spiritual guide to explain the strange landscapes and bizarre features of my subjective world, all these outer X's were like solid markers inscribed on the concrete surface of the objective world, providing touchstones in conventional reality for what became an increasingly esoteric inner journey home.

Over time, my trust in the X grew. I even made a game of it back then, toying with the idea that the universe was sending me signs along the way, reassuring me that X did indeed "mark the spot," and that my search for the hidden treasure of enlightenment was not in vain.

As my confidence grew, I began exploring this subtle form with greater degrees of involvement and curiosity. Initially there was no consistency in the following ability, but I eventually discovered that I could intentionally make the X reappear whenever I wanted it to by recalling it from memory. And the more I did, the more it began to behave in an even more sublime way.

At first, the following process only happened occasionally, but in the final months leading up to my awakening, the X became such a constant presence in my field of vision that its transformational effect was available almost continuously. If I kept my attention fixed on the X long enough, pulses of pearly light would flow down the four axes towards its center, and as I followed this influx of light, my attention would get pulled into the central point where all four glowing lines intersect.

Next, my consciousness would pass through the nexus, followed by a brilliant flash of white light that flooded the entire field of my vision. When my perception of reality returned, everything was infused with a feeling of oneness.

During these moments of nondual perception, inside and outside were no longer separate from one another. The subtle boundary that normally divided my sense of self from reality dissolved. In fact, all conventional sense of having an identity would fall away. There was no self.

Instead, the entire field of my awareness became totally transparent to the oneness of everything. My vision merged with the world I observed, both becoming one vast and unified expression of the same omnipresent consciousness that gave rise to my own luminous gaze looking upon it.

During these moments, I knew that I was experiencing a clear, undistorted view of the true nature of reality, and that this was the same expanded state of awareness I had elicited throughout my childhood. What's more, because I was older, I felt more confident repeating this discovery.

Yet, as wonderful as these nondual moments were, the immense clarity of seeing things this way still wouldn't hold. Eventually the oneness of everything would dissipate, and my consciousness would return to a dualistic mode of perception. It was only after my awakening that this divided view was finally undone, replaced by a more permanent state of nondual realization.

Chapter 11

My Search Continues at University

MY SPIRITUAL INQUIRY PROCEEDED during the spring and summer months following my first year of university. I continued my writing forays and studying Dewdney's work for sources of inspiration and insight.

One field of research that Dewdney draws upon to communicate his poetic vision is Geology. By following up references in his poetry, I learned about a theory in evolutionary biology called *punctuated equilibrium*, which proposes that the evolution of new species occurs in rapid events first, followed by the more gradual process of natural selection described and popularized by Charles Darwin.

My worldview was still materialistic during this period, so the fact that sudden bursts of evolutionary change could theoretically occur in physical organisms allowed me to consider the possibility that a similar leap of personal evolution could occur in me.

Not in my physical body, but rather in my mind. I hoped to achieve a rapid and radical inner change, a quantum leap in consciousness if you will, that would lead to a permanent shift into the nondual state of awareness that I was striving to attain.

Although I no longer remembered that this endeavor was related to the deeper purpose of my life, I felt motivated to achieve this spiritual transformation for the benefit of others. If I was successful, I thought to myself at the time, then I could show others how to attain it, too.

Without realizing it, I was pursuing what is known as the *Bodhisattva* ideal in Buddhism, which stresses attaining enlightenment in order to liberate others, in contrast to other paths that focus solely on personal salvation.

After the summer ended, I returned for my second year of university. Once again I selected courses that I felt would aid my spiritual inquiry. I chose Creative Writing, Linguistics, Philosophy of Language, Postmodern Literary Criticism, and Astronomy.

I was interested in studying the most recent scientific theories about the creation of the cosmos and selected astronomy to add to the growing body of knowledge supporting my inner quest.

As a result of my studies during my first year, I became even more fascinated with language itself, and concluded that it played a critical role in preventing a person from accessing the perception of oneness that I was pursuing. I reasoned that since words are what we use to describe reality, then perhaps it was possible to discover the pure essence below the surface of reality by deconstructing language itself.

My motivation was like that of a physicist trying to get to the quantum level of reality. In the same way that physicists pry matter apart to find out what it is made of and where it comes from, I thought that if I could break language down into its rudimentary parts, I might be able to gain a glimpse of the same mysterious substance beneath the phenomenal world.

Alongside this effort, I developed an interest in understanding the postmodern worldview, which I had been exposed to for the first time soon after entering university. I figured that the leading edge of philosophical thought in the West ought to have something important to say about this whole business of understanding the true nature of reality. I wanted to know if there was a final answer or way of explaining reality that would allow me to feel like I finally "got it" and thus resolve my search for the absolute truth. I had high hopes that postmodern philosophy would provide this. What a surprise to learn that the postmodern worldview is based on the philosophical position that such knowledge is prohibited from human experience. Stated briefly, the postmodern stance is that all knowledge is socially constructed and that there is nowhere you can go to gain a bird's-eye view of the way things really are.

I was deeply affected by the sense of meaninglessness left inside me as a result of postmodern thought and academic life in general. According to the academic world, the search for any absolute truth or ultimate meaning in life is considered intellectually naïve, nothing more than a comforting story to stave off the underlying sense of existential malaise at the heart of the human condition.

Yet, I knew there was a way to understand the true nature of reality based on an awareness of the oneness of everything. I'd personally experienced this mode of knowing repeatedly throughout my life. Not only had I experienced it constantly throughout my childhood, I was re-experiencing it during this period of my life more frequently, primarily due to the appearance and effect of the luminous X.

In order to escape from the mental web of philosophical abstractions and finally resolve my search, I concluded that something truly profound was required: to become one with the source of existence. I no longer equated this metaphysical dimension with God, nor did I know if it was even knowable experientially, but I was determined to find out.

I had serious doubts about this endeavor at the time. It occurred to me that my pursuit to encounter a primordial dimension could be a total waste of time at best, and at worst actually harmful psychologically. To exacerbate things, in the final months leading up to the night of my awakening, I began to suffer from a well-known existential problem. I became painfully aware of the fact that I was fundamentally separate from other people. This insight troubled me deeply. I realized that no matter how much I improved the way I related with others, I was, and always would be, completely separate from everyone else.

As a result of this insight, I began losing interest in being around people, and often sank into an abysmal state of sadness. Sometimes my feelings of isolation got so bad that my whole being would feel drenched in sorrow. During the deepest pits of despair, the only way I could find a bit of relief was to think about all the misery in the world and willingly open myself up to feeling all that pain in heartbreaking sympathy with my own. This widened the focus of my concern beyond my own suffering and reminded me that I was working on solving the problem of human suffering in general. But, for the most part, the last few months prior to my awakening was one long dark night of the soul.

Chapter 12

The Night of My Awakening

I T HAPPENED ON a bitterly cold winter night. I had just returned from a vacation to Florida that I took with my girlfriend
at the time. The trip was a gift from my mother, intended to
alleviate some of my existential sadness.

Earlier that same night, my friend Jackson called me on
the phone and asked me to join him at a local restaurant bar.
I was not too interested in going out, but it had been a while
since Jackson and I had hung out together, and he eventually
persuaded me to join him by offering to drive.

I brought pictures of my trip. We were both interested in
astronomy at the time, and I had visited the Kennedy Space
Center while in Florida. We sat at the bar looking at the pictures while I related details and shared stories. Meanwhile,
an older woman sitting nearby, probably in her late forties,
kept glancing over. I could sense she was lonely and wanted
some company, so I invited her to join us.

She was a good listener and enjoyed my storytelling, but
Jackson was not comfortable with this new situation. I knew
he was thinking that I was being a pushover by inviting this
woman to join us, but my heart really went out to her.

A few minutes later, Jackson found a reason to excuse himself. A couple of people he knew showed up, and he seized
the opportunity to go over and talk with them.

I continued showing my pictures to this woman, sharing
the remaining stories from my trip, occasionally looking over
at Jackson. I caught a few snippets of their conversation, just
enough to know they were making fun of the fact that I was
sitting at the bar talking with an older lady. We talked a bit
more about my girlfriend and life in general, then I politely
said goodnight and wished her well.

I made my way over to the group of people Jackson was with and punched him in the arm for being inconsiderate, especially since the woman was close enough to hear them laughing and could have thought they were laughing at her.

I waited a few more minutes, just long enough to gracefully suggest to Jackson that we get going. He agreed somewhat reluctantly. We said goodbye to the people in the group, then made our way to the parking lot.

We sat in the car for ten minutes or so, waiting for the engine to warm up. Jackson wanted to do something else, but I wasn't interested. I was put off by what happened inside.

The car ride back to my house was a quiet one. As he pulled up to the end of my driveway, Jackson put the car in park so that we could talk a bit more. It was extremely cold that night, so he left the car running to keep the heat on.

With the hum of the engine idling in the background, we spoke about trivial things and joked around a bit. I eventually brought up the woman from the bar and expressed my concern for her.

Without directly accusing Jackson of being uncompassionate, I emphasized that we should be more caring towards others, especially when they are so obviously suffering from loneliness.

"Don't you feel the least bit sorry for her?" I asked.

"Why should I?" he fired back defensively.

"Because she needed some company and we happened to be there. You could have hung out for a bit longer and just been present with her."

"Forget that. I had a long week at work and my idea of kicking back and cracking some jokes over a beer doesn't include some desperate woman looking to join our party. Let her find her own friends. Besides, you're so blind and naïve you couldn't tell that all she really wanted was for you to take her home and have sex with her."

I laughed at his little jab, but I was serious, and I wanted him to be, too. "I was showing her pictures of my trip with my girlfriend! I'm telling you she was lonely and just wanted someone to talk to. Besides, if you knew she was looking for a little loving, why didn't *you* go for it? It's been a while since you've gotten any action, Jackson."

He laughed at my comeback, and we continued our back and forth a bit more, jabbing each other playfully. But the more we got into it, the more impassioned I became. I started lecturing him about all the layers of bullshit that prevent us from making a simple heart-to-heart connection with other people, especially strangers.

To illustrate my point, I gestured tearing pieces of body armor off my chest. Surprisingly, as I was doing this, inwardly I saw two riveted iron plates covering my innermost self, and as I pantomimed peeling these armored plates off, the liberating spaciousness of my true nature revealed itself for a brief moment.

I wanted both Jackson and myself to transcend the feeling of separation from others, but my impassioned plea left a completely different impression on him. He became pensive and morose. I immediately felt badly about it and told him to forget everything I said and called it a night. As I swung the door shut, I said we'd talk again soon.

On my way towards my house, I heard Jackson roll down the passenger window and call out to me. I looked back as he yelled out some last little jab that I don't remember, and I responded in kind.

Chapter 13

The Moment of Enlightenment

T HE WALK FROM THE CAR to my house was a short one, but it was so cold that night that I was freezing by the time I reached the front door. Shivering, I turned the doorknob as quietly as possible, trying not to wake my parents. I heard my mother get up and followed the sound of her footsteps as she walked across the upstairs hallway.

"It's just me, Mom," I whispered in anticipation, as she made her way to the top of the stairwell.

"Oh, Stephen, thank God you're home," she said with a deep sigh. "I was worried. I wish you would call me when you know you're going to be out so late. You have no idea how hard it is for me to fall asleep when I don't know where you kids are. You know how I worry."

It was a familiar phrase to which I replied with my usual ineffective reassurance. "You don't need to worry about me, Mom. I'm fine. Go back to bed. Love you."

"Okay, sweetie. Love you, too."

I went to the living room, sunk into the sofa, and turned the TV on. I stared blankly at the images on the tube, lost in thought. A short while later, I rolled onto my back and stared at the ceiling, letting my awareness widen into witnessing – the deeper state of mind that had become such a predominant presence in my search for enlightenment.

I began reviewing the various lines of my inquiry, which coalesced into an intensified longing for truth, for liberation, for final understanding. This prompted a subtle phenomenon to emerge.

I saw my thoughts coming up from the depths of my subconscious mind. On the surface, they were passing by like a train made of words all chugging along to create the meaning of my musings. At the same time, I could see each thought rising up from the subconscious depths, gathering various ideas, images, and associations stored in the data banks of memory.

I also had the ability to trace my thoughts back to their source by following them down to where they began. Once there, I found another subtle form of consciousness, which I implicitly recognized as an unmodified thought-form, or the anatomical mechanism that enables human thinking.

This structure was composed of two spheres – one black and one white – connected to each other by a single tube. I had actually followed a series of these "binary seeds" below the surface of my thinking mind, my attention moving down a kind of polarity ladder that shrank in size the farther down I went. At the very base of each of these ladders, I could see the place where all thoughts are born in the mind.

Looking across a formless field of mental energy, I saw an assembly line of these binary structures. They were waiting as potential thought-forms, marching dutifully like an army of worker ants ready to climb up through the tunnels of thinking in order to gather and generate meaning.

As this was happening, I knew that I was observing how thoughts and language function together in the human mind, which provided perceptual evidence for some of the musings that had informed the linguistic lines of my spiritual inquiry.

In the midst of this subtle mode of perception, my Mom stepped into the room. She said she was worried about my well-being, adding that she had been woken up by some bad dreams. Then she placed her hand on my forehead to check my temperature, a skill she had refined so well that she could instantly determine if a visit to the hospital was necessary or not. "Sweetie, you're burning up," she said with urgency.

I had warmed up pretty quickly after coming in from the cold, but I did not feel unwell. I felt a bit disoriented from the strange effects that were occurring in my consciousness, but I implicitly knew that the rise in my body temperature was not due to any physical illness. I surmised that the bizarre effects I was witnessing were most likely the reason for the rise in my body temperature.

Although I didn't know this at the time, extreme bodily heat is a well-known phenomenon that often occurs in people when they undergo the same sort of spiritual transformation I experienced on this night. All I knew for sure was that my mind was moving into some strange new territory, and yet, I trusted that whatever was happening was for the best.

"It's okay, Mom," I said reassuringly. "I know I'm hot, but I'm fine. I'll call you if I feel worse, but I'm okay for now."

After she left, I closed my eyes and turned my attention inward again, eager to continue watching the subtle machinery churning out the thoughts in my mind. Luckily, the same noetic perception was still available. So I kept going back and forth, from the top to the bottom, following my thoughts on the surface down to where they began as binary seeds below.

Eventually, the display dissipated, and I was left feeling absolutely certain about two things.

First, I understood that the primal state of every conceivable thought is nothing more than a play of opposites, and that the basis of the thinking mind to generate the meaning of one thing depends on the cognition of its opposite to create the necessary contrast for meaning to occur. And second, at an even deeper level of insight, I understood that this black and white object was a primordial form of polarized energy that reflected the principal of duality operating throughout creation.

This second insight led to an epiphany. I realized that the numinous experience I was seeking could never be found in any thoughts, words, or ideas about the source of existence. No matter how profoundly or accurately conceptual knowledge expresses the indivisible mystery at the heart of creation, there is no mental substitute or equivalent for actually experiencing the source of existence. And more than anything else, I wanted to become one with that primordial dimension.

Feeling something huge was approaching, I went downstairs to my bedroom in the basement. I stretched out on my mattress and waited, alert. The room was pitch black. I dropped even deeper into witnessing, and once again I began contemplating the koan: *If I can be aware of myself as a looker, then who or what is this aspect of my awareness that is always looking?*

Finally, after months of self-inquiry and contemplation, a response to this question spontaneously emerged, though not in any form I ever would have anticipated or imagined. An unfathomable Presence filled my room. It was too dark to see it, but I definitely sensed its sublime magnificence all around me. It felt vast and eternal.

Then, using a mode of communication more direct than telepathy, the Presence conveyed that it was my inquiry that had summoned its appearance. It then proceeded to communicate something else directly into my mind without the need for words. It impressed upon me that if I wanted to reach the final goal of my spiritual quest, I had to fully surrender to the vast nothingness I felt all around me.

While considering the implications of what this act of surrender entailed, a familiar form flashed before my mind's eye. It was the X. It was only visible for a split second, just long enough for me to recognize it as such, before it transformed into another form: a luminous weblike structure.

This new subtle form looked like a computer-generated vortex, which I admired for the geometric simplicity and beauty of its design. It was clearly a gateway, but to where or what exactly, I had no idea.

As I stared into this glowing vortex, I got the distinct impression that what the Presence meant by complete surrender was to let go of everything and plunge into this portal. This was accompanied by a powerful urge from the Presence that wanted me to stop resisting and let go.

I was actually quite hesitant because I had no idea if this Presence was a benevolent force or not. Subjectively, it felt like being at the edge of a black hole that was about to pull me into oblivion.

My heart started beating wildly, slamming against the inside of my chest. Throbs of blood pumped through my veins, filling my body with a primal fear far deeper and even more instinctual than the biological instinct to survive.

I knew deep within that if I allowed myself to plunge into the vortex, I would surely die the ultimate death. Not necessarily the death of my physical body, though that seemed possible. It was more of an existential death. Everything I could possibly identify with as "me" would die.

I paused for a moment to reflect on what was happening and to try to slow things down a bit. I'd clearly reached a critical crossroad on my path and knew an important decision had to be made. But I had no idea if the right way forward was to pull away from this vortex or plunge into it. It could have been a gateway to the very source of existence I'd been striving for, although I had my doubts.

I had no context for understanding any of this. No map of the inner terrain of enlightenment. No conceptual framework to predict the various stages of awakening. It was all a complete mystery to me. My knowledge of the path was unfolding with each step I took. As a result, I had no idea what would happen if I surrendered, and I wasn't sure that I was ready to give up my very sense of existence in order to find out what would happen next.

In an attempt to buy some more time before making a final decision, I asked myself whether this was all occurring in my head or if this vortex had actually manifested in the darkened space of my bedroom.

Responding to my attempt to delay what was unfolding, the Presence revealed that trying to make such a distinction was unnecessary and that the only way to find out the answer to this or any other question I had was to surrender.

I continued staring into the gaping void, no longer able to ascertain if this subtle form was only appearing inside my mind's eye, or if an actual portal had opened up in the middle of my room, while at the same time knowing that it didn't matter. All that really mattered was to make the right choice.

There was no indication from the Presence either way. Inwardly, I hoped that the vortex would lead to the source of existence, but there was no guidance given from the Presence whether it would take me there, nor what the consequence of such an experience would be even if it did.

The extreme nature of the situation, combined with my lack of knowing, made my mind reel. Give up my very sense of existence in order to find the source of existence? It was so paradoxical. And the consequences seemed drastic if things turned out otherwise.

I hesitated for one last second, then finally figured that no matter what happened, the result would surely turn out better than continuing to live in the overall state of apathy I was in at the time. So I stopped resisting and let go.

Chapter 14

Into the Void

A s I ENTERED THE VORTEX, my egoic self disintegrated. It happened instantaneously through a profound change in the subtle structures supporting my personal identity. The mirror in the back of my mind turned 180 degrees and moved in front of me.

Pulled forward by the force of descent, I smashed through this mirror, which sent all the shards into the abyss I was falling into. Seconds later, everything went completely quiet, and the sensation of falling stopped.

The pause gave me a moment to reflect on what had just happened. Every remnant of my personal identity was gone, obliterated. It was like amnesia, but even that fails to convey the sense of emptiness fully. It felt like I'd never existed.

There was nothing. No more life. No more memories. No more me. Nothing. All that remained was my disembodied awareness and this endless realm of nothingness – a vacuum devoid of any features, forms, or qualities. No formless bliss. No absolute truth. Nothing.

A line of questioning arose from the hollowed out space of my being. Had I made some sort of fatal spiritual error by allowing myself to be swallowed up by this strange maw of nonexistence? And if so, was the consequence for making the wrong choice that I was doomed to spend the rest of eternity in this limbolike existence of nothingness?

A response to both questions arose in the form of another change of state. From within the very depths of this blank enigma, everything suddenly shifted and quickly improved. Right away I knew the foreboding Presence that initiated my descent into this endless realm of nothingness was actually a benevolent force orchestrating this mystical journey for my highest good. The radical emptying of my consciousness and the annihilation of my egoic self was a necessary preparation for what came next.

First, my consciousness expanded beyond all divisions of "existence" and "nonexistence" and became one with the very source of creation. Here, all notions of separateness united in a boundless dimension beyond description that I immediately realized was the primordial, unmanifested realm of absolute nothingness that existed before the big bang. The moment I merged with this original metaphysical dimension, I knew it was also the formless wellspring out of which everything in existence is constantly emerging.

Next, I heard a voice that belonged to the Presence. It had a majestic power that simply declared, "I AM." Upon hearing this declaration, I knew that I was witnessing the original face of God.

It wasn't until many years after this experience that I started referring to this transcendental reality as God, due to all the usual associations that diminish the grandiosity and mystery of the Creator of the Universe. Yet, in that moment, I knew without naming it as such that I had, in fact, attained a complete and total union with God – the one and eternal Supreme Being.

Next, I apprehended that this boundless dimension was omnipresent in all things as their true identity, including my own. I understood, once and for all, that at the very pinnacle of self-awareness, we can reunite with this infinite and formless Presence or Identity known universally as I AM. I also realized that my ability to stay connected to this transcendental level of self-realization was firmly established.

I felt deeply humbled and grateful for how unconditionally loving God was for allowing this union to take place. All was revealed so freely. What's more, God continued unfolding the significance of this formless dimension, adding more knowledge to my understanding.

Next, I saw how the energy of creation and consciousness are inextricably linked, generating our life experiences. As a result of this knowledge, I appreciated how everything I had experienced in my own life came about as a result of whatever was inside me that needed to happen.

I also understood that the formless source of everything had always existed and would continue to exist forever. This meant that ultimately there is no such thing as death in any permanent sense. In addition, I saw that the formless essence of the human soul exists beyond all space and time and never dies. This last revelation was the same one I had discovered as a child, and upon rediscovering it in early adulthood, I lost all fear of death.

Chapter 15

Returning to the World

I FOUND WHAT I'D BEEN searching for. Deep within I always knew that this dimension was discoverable, and the result of finding it felt like the culmination of my spiritual journey. Feeling like I'd found all the answers I'd been searching for and so much more, I rested in a blissful state of perfect peace and transcendental knowing that seemed to last forever.

At some point during this timeless sojourn, I received another message, again without words. A choice needed to be made. I could stay in this formless realm forever. Or, return to my life in the physical world of form.

I was certain that I wouldn't lose my connection to this formless dimension if I chose the latter. And so, knowing it would still be accessible, I decided to come back.

The moment I did, the same majestic voice that revealed itself as I AM whispered a final parting request: "Tell others."

This message was accompanied by an almost joking, yet warmly reassuring feeling, as if to say, "Not so fast. One last thing before you go. Although this won't be easy, I know you can do it…"

Upon hearing this message, I knew I'd have to share my realization of enlightenment with others one day, a task that also made me recall my life's purpose to help people awaken their true nature. What's more, the moment I acknowledged that this was my destiny, I was filled with a powerful and reassuring impression that humanity is on the verge of undergoing a collective transformation and spiritual awakening.

Several years would pass before I felt ready to tell others about any of this. It was so mind-boggling that it took a few years before I could even begin to comprehend much of it, and there was still more that happened.

As soon as I decided to return to my life, another series of events occurred.

First, I remembered being in this same dimension prior to incarnating, which is when I recalled choosing my parents. As this memory came back to me, my current immersion in the formless dimension began to subside. But instead of falling from the highest plane of existence this time around, I felt myself rising up from the groundless ground of being.

During this ascension, another process took place in tandem that lifted and transformed my entire identity. A mass of scintillating gems rose up around me, lifting the shards from the mirror in my mind that had shattered at the beginning of this mystical odyssey.

I believe these gems were from the cosmic chandelier that had descended into my being a year or so before, now reactivated and coordinating this rapid ascension of my soul.

Once again, these gems formed into the shape of another pyramid, only this time it was inverted and composed solely of diamonds. These crystal forms functioned like holograms that were encoded with all the memories from my life, and as they rose up around me, I had 360 degree vision.

The combined effect allowed me to see and understand the true meaning and value of my life. It was instantaneous, like watching hundreds of films fast-forwarded, each movie replaying a significant segment of my life.

The karmic significance of everything I'd ever thought, felt, said, or done up until this point in my life became perfectly clear. I saw exactly which actions in my life had either hindered or facilitated the journey of my soul back home.

I also saw how every action in my life had affected those around me, including all the joy and suffering I had caused in others. At the same time, whether positive or negative, I understood that all these experiences contained a necessary lesson that had to be learned, either for myself or for others – and often both.

As part of this same soul ascending radical change, all the unresolved experiences (sanskaras) in my subconscious mind were resurrected and reassembled into a more integrated configuration, ultimately releasing me from the karma stored in them, while raising the location of my identity into a higher plane of being.

The overall result of this transformation lifted and then fused the entire field of my consciousness and awareness with my higher self. Subjectively, it felt like the mirror in the back of my mind became a vast window above my head that opened up to the formless, timeless, and boundless space of I AM.

All this took place in a matter of seconds. As it was happening, I was simultaneously aware that I was basically undergoing the afterlife phenomenon known as a *life review*. I also knew that I was going through this process in a fairly generic way, almost entirely free of any religious or cultural reference points.

For me, it felt like I was standing before the court of my higher self, acting as both judge and jury of my own actions in life. And even though the willingness to accept all responsibility came easily and seemed the most natural way to allow the process to complete itself, I also realized that it could have been far more difficult if I had resisted.

As soon as it was over, I was struck by the notion that this process – a descent into the Void followed by a life review – occurs at the end of everyone's life, and that this is not always an easy thing for the human soul to go through.

This realization so moved me that it became one of the most powerful driving forces behind my current dedication to help people make progress on their spiritual path in this lifetime and also assist them during the transition into the **spirit world** at the end of this life.

After everything was over, I went to bed and slept like a baby. The following day my parents discovered that the foundation wall supporting the entire front of our house had split down the middle sometime during the night.

I said nothing about my experience. However, deep within I knew it was more than a mere coincidence. I realize how preposterous it may sound to suggest this, but I'm certain that the Presence of God combined with everything that had happened to me must have charged the basement with so much spiritual and psychic energy that it physically caused the concrete in the wall to crack in half.

Of course, there are natural causes that could have explained this fracture, but one thing you learn to appreciate on the spiritual path is both the timing and symbolic meaning of seemingly unrelated events. And just like the foundation of the house, the substructure of my entire identity had been broken wide open by God.

What's also interesting is that the structural engineer who assessed the situation said he'd never seen anything like it before. The damage was so significant the wall had to be dug up and replaced. Fortunately, the townhouse complex covered the cost so the repairs didn't burden my parents financially; otherwise, I would have felt extra guilty for not being able to explain why I believed it was my fault.

Chapter 16

The Aftermath

F ROM BEGINNING TO END, my awakening experience only lasted about ten minutes, although it felt much longer. When I woke up the next morning, I implicitly knew what had happened. I'd been brought into a state of complete unity with the very source of existence and was totally transformed by it.

I called my friend, Jackson, and asked him to come over right away, explaining that I had something important to tell him that I couldn't share over the phone. Once he arrived, I tried to communicate the nature of my experience from the night before, but it was all too paradoxical to describe in any adequate way. I ended up stammering as I struggled to find the words before realizing it was pointless.

After that, I remained almost completely silent about the entire event for years. Inwardly, however, I focused on deepening my understanding of the transformation I underwent in order to help stabilize it.

The first thing I noticed was that I was existing on a transcendental level of being. My consciousness had been lifted into a higher plane, far above my former one. It was shocking to discover that the location of my new self was no longer in my body; instead, it hovered mysteriously above my head.

I also noticed a distinct lack of desire to change or manipulate anything that went on in the world of form down below. I still dealt with whatever needed to be dealt with, and cared for whatever needed my care, but beyond that, I had no desire for any new experiences to feel fulfilled. The ineffable bliss of enlightened awareness was all that I wanted or needed.

In the weeks that followed, I began to notice all sorts of other changes, as well. One of the most striking differences was that all the maladaptive thoughts, emotions, and desires that had occasionally occupied my attention or influenced my behavior prior to this awakening were gone, miraculously replaced by beneficial states of mind, speech, and action.

The disintegration and restructuring of my egoic self also gave me far more control and flexibility over my personality, allowing me to act in whatever way I saw fit, based on the circumstances of almost any situation.

My interactions with people also began to take on a felt depth of meaning and emotional connection that I had only known in special moments previously. Even the most insignificant exchanges felt charged with a joyous quality.

At the same time, no matter what happened, whether positive or negative, I was equally undisturbed, at peace with the way things unfolded.

Because I stopped desiring for life to go in any particular way, what would have typically been a source of frustration for me in the past was now regarded dispassionately as just another appearance or phenomenon, a ripple on the surface of the oneness of reality.

This feeling of oneness was based on the realization that the same formless dimension that I'd always known to be my true nature was the original essence of everyone and everything in existence. And since it was all an expression of the same underlying source, it was all manifesting exactly as it was meant to, no matter how seemingly magical, pleasant, frustrating, mundane, painful, or trivial it appeared to be.

This perspective altered my perception so radically that a pristine clarity of seeing emerged that revealed the true nature of reality as perpetually nondual. Everything became illuminated, a unified and radiant display of one underlying formless source of existence that I was now one with.

Chapter 17

A New and Disciplined Lifestyle

T HE MORNING IMMEDIATELY following my awakening I knew that I had to make drastic changes in my life to stabilize this new level of self-realization.

Physically, I was unhealthy and overweight. To fix this, a flood of inspiration and healing energy descended into my body, along with an unswerving will and implicit knowledge of how to adopt a more balanced and wholesome lifestyle.

I had been raised on a fairly healthy diet, but even with all the good eating habits that had been inherited, I saw how most of these foods were not right for me anymore. Also, my eating habits had become fairly unwholesome during university. I had grown accustomed to living on fast food, coffee, and cigarettes.

To get healthy, I began running every day and doing yoga. I also adopted a strictly vegan diet and removed many impurities from my life. To help cleanse my system, I began fasting periodically and drank only pure, distilled water.

During this period, I had the good fortune of finding an excellent yoga teacher, Mar Jean, though she preferred being called "M." She taught a drop-in class as part of the student services program at York University.

The beneficial effects of doing yoga were manifold. I had been suffering from sciatica for several months, which went away soon after beginning to practice. As I learned to execute the postures (asanas) my teacher introduced, I found I could hold most of the positions for any length of time. Those that were more difficult, mainly due to various tensions or aches and pains in parts of my body, I learned to heal and release using breath control (pranayama). And, of course, I rediscovered the joy of breathing from my belly again.

The results of my new diet, yoga regimen, and running were outwardly noticeable. I lost forty pounds in a matter of weeks. As each day passed, more body fat melted away. The changes in my lifestyle helped this cleansing process along, but it was the healing vibrations coursing through my body that made it happen so quickly. I was on fire with the energies of enlightenment.

When it was finished, my body weight returned to what it was in my early teens, at the prime of my youth. Admittedly, I looked like an emaciated yogi, and I eventually returned to a more normal weight years later, but during this time it was necessary to shed all the fat from my body to assist the transformations that were simultaneously taking place on all the other levels of my being.

Although I told no one about what had happened to me on the night of my awakening, friends and family members were curious about the reason for all the changes in my lifestyle. For a few weeks, my mother was convinced that I had developed anorexia, but I assured her that everything I was doing was beneficial for my health.

As a result of all the changes taking place, my whole being began radiating a purer energy than I had ever known or felt before. As I became leaner and cleaner, the essence of enlightenment began to move more fully throughout my entire being, transmuting my body, heart, and mind.

The results were profound.

I no longer identified with my body. I hadn't dissociated. In fact, I was more aware of my heart beating, blood flowing, lungs breathing, and so on. But when I really tuned into my body, I found and felt that it had essentially disappeared. In retrospect, I now know that it was transformed by the formless presence of nondual being. This made my body feel like an empty shell at first, and then later on, a kind of lens that embodies the endless awareness of the awakened state.

My heart opened up to all that is. Universal love for everyone and everything in existence became my constant emotional state of being. As for personal feelings or desires, they rarely arose. But even if they did, I was content to watch them ripple away like tiny waves passing over a pool when a stone disturbs its motionless rest.

Finally, my mind was transformed into a limitless medium for whatever arises in consciousness. At the same time, all the mental activity normally associated with interpreting life simply ceased to inhabit my inner world. And because my mind was no longer busy analyzing anything, I actually stopped dreaming while asleep.

To help stabilize these developments, I adopted a yogic asana called *death pose* for my sleeping position, and for the next few years spent my nights abiding in the formlessness of dreamless being.

During the ascetic phase following my awakening

Chapter 18

A Symbolic Funeral Pyre

A FEW DAYS AFTER the night of my awakening, I decided to burn everything I had written related to my spiritual journey. Altogether, there were probably a few thousand pages' worth.

This material was a loose collection of stuff mostly containing spiritual reflections on life in the form of short aphorisms and syllogisms. It also included mini essays, snippets of dreams and my analyses of them, details about some nonordinary experiences of mine, stream-of-consciousness writing and a bunch of other experimental creative writing pieces, plus the short stories I wrote during high school.

I decided to burn these pages as a way of practically and ritually saying goodbye to my former identity. I realize now that they contained a lot of interesting information about my personal journey, but at the time it represented my "old self" and way of being in the world, and burning this material was an act of nonattachment and an abandonment of that former "false" identity.

It was wintertime but it was so unseasonably warm that day that it felt more like autumn. I went into my backyard to build a fire for this private ceremony, using a metal waste bin for the cremation. I lit a few pieces to get the fire going, adding more as the flames allowed. Within minutes, I was dropping stacks of paper in, watching dispassionately as reams of my writing turned into smoke and ashes.

I stood there gazing at the fire contemplatively, an activity I've always enjoyed. After a while, I noticed something strange about the smoke. It went up in a perfectly straight line. The subtlest current of air could have altered its ascent, yet nothing occurred to disturb it.

I wasn't overly interested in this phenomenon at first, so I kept feeding pages into the fire. Meanwhile, this thin pillar of smoke continued rising steadily into the sky without wavering. But then something so odd came on the scene that I had to pay attention.

A bunch of crows started cawing in the distance. At first, I could only hear them, but they soon appeared, and in great numbers. The first flock flew over the townhouses to my left, then more flew in from the right, until they were converging from every direction, forming a massive flock overhead. I'd never seen so many crows at the same time, but it seemed as though every crow in the surrounding area had gathered to participate in this rookery.

My first thought was that they were on their way somewhere else, but they were clearly gathering in the sky directly above me. Plus, as their numbers increased, they exhibited an uncanny level of shared intention. They began flying in concentric circles of clockwise and counterclockwise flight patterns, forming what amounted to a huge, swirling vortex in the sky.

They continued flying in this highly co-ordinated fashion for about ten minutes or so. Then, at a certain point, they altered their flight pattern once more. Most of the crows left the vortex and perched themselves on the top edge of a high-rise condominium building nearby, where they watched the other crows still flying in formation.

These remaining crows, about a dozen or so, maintained a single circle high in the sky. Occasionally, two or three of them would leave the circle and join the larger group on the building. Amazingly, as they approached, cawing and maybe even communicating telepathically, replacements readily took flight to join the turning circle in the sky.

What was equally fascinating was how precisely they had positioned themselves in relation to the fire I was tending to down below. They were directly above it. I could tell because the perimeter of their circular flight path was perpendicular with the spot where the pillar of smoke disappeared into the atmosphere.

With all these crows flying around with what seemed to be such a clear purpose and intent, I couldn't help but wonder what it all meant. Were they aware of what had happened to me? My first inclination was to dismiss the thought, figuring that their aerial display was just an instinctual reaction to the fire, but it was way too elaborate to accept this conclusion.

Next, I considered the possibility that there was, in fact, a message in their flight pattern, and if so, what it might be. The scene certainly spoke to me in a symbolic way. The vortex reminded me of going into the Void, and the circle seemed to aptly reflect the higher orbit of my consciousness, with the pillar of smoke possibly indicating the energetic connection linking my higher self to my physical body.

I finished feeding the remaining pages into the fire, periodically looking up at the iridescent black birds majestically circling overhead. After everything was burnt, they all began dispersing. At first, more than half left at the same time. Then groups of three or four broke away from those that remained, until the last few finally flew away.

As strange and striking as this event was, a few months later the same structure – a vortex – appeared twice more, only this time it wasn't composed of crows. Instead, the same spiraling form manifested first as a mini-tornado, then in the mysterious lights of the aurora borealis, and both on the same day. I'll describe the circumstances surrounding these events in the next chapter.

Leaving University & Working in the Bush

M Y SPIRITUAL TRANSFORMATION occurred in the middle of my second year of university. I finished off the final semester in the spring of 1996, then took a leave of absence.

I planned to return and complete my degree in the future, but after my awakening, my focus shifted towards stabilizing my true nature, which required doing activities that engaged my whole being. So, I got a job in forestry planting trees.

I chose this type of work knowing it was an ideal way to both strengthen and challenge myself physically, emotionally, mentally, and spiritually, while also earning some money.

I was really attracted to the mental discipline required to plant trees all day long because it was an excellent way to practice an active form of meditation that I'll explain at the end of this chapter. Also, living outdoors and working in the bush, I knew, would test the stability of my emotional detachment, which is needed to sustain the awakened state. And finally, I was curious to see how far I could push myself physically in light of my body's newfound strength and endurance.

I was hired by a private company on a contractual basis. The job began in early May and was scheduled to end by the first week of July, or when all the trees in the spring contract were planted. The possibility of extending this contract into the summer existed for anyone who became a "high quality" tree planter.

To add another challenge to my list, I decided to see if I could become an eligible candidate, even though we were told that very few first-timers are offered summer employment.

It took two days of travel to reach our first destination, a township in northwestern Ontario called Atikokan. We were scheduled to start planting in some nearby logging areas first, followed by Northern Manitoba or Saskatchewan, and then British Columbia, the latter opportunity made available only for those tree planters who were offered summer contracts.

On the first day of work, we were trained to fight forest fires. Part of our contract stated that we could be outsourced to help the Ministry of Natural Resources fight forest fires in the vicinity if our services were needed.

We went to an area that had been clear-cut. All the trees in the forest had been cut down, yet only those of commercial value removed. The remaining trees were burned in order to clear the area so it could be replanted with a single species for more economical harvesting later on.

When a forest is slashed and burned in this way, fires will sometimes continue smoldering under the earth in the roots of the trees, and these underground fires can actually spread into uncut areas and spawn new forest fires.

The way to stop these underground fires from spreading is to dig a trench around the perimeter of the suspected area where the fire is thought to be burning below the ground.

That day, we practiced digging these trenches as part of a co-ordinated team effort. We were taken through a drill and dug a fairly small perimeter around an arbitrarily designated area chosen for this exercise. Then, surprisingly, an actual fire spontaneously combusted nearby, and suddenly our simulated drill became real.

We rushed to the area where the fire was burning above ground. A massive tree stump that had been heavily charred by the previous slash-and-burn fire erupted again. Fueled by the wind, the flames threatened to spread into an uncut area nearby. Everyone started digging for hot spots, evidenced by glowing embers in the root structure.

After several minutes of searching frantically, we finally found the source of the subterranean blaze and dug a trench around it to stop the cindering roots from spreading.

This emergency exhilarated the entire crew, prompting lots of excited banter as we all decompressed from the surge of adrenalin. While outwardly engaged in the fun, I amused myself with the thought that if hell actually existed, it might look similar to this place.

The landscape was depressing. Massive fallen trees were strewn one on top of another like a giant-sized game of pick-up sticks. The ground was mostly exposed rock dotted with small pockets of a two-inch layer of peat and humus, a mixture that could hardly be called soil. Finding suitable places to plant trees required climbing and crawling over and under these charred logs, and then striking the rocky surface with a shovel, feeling for soil deep enough to secure the seedlings.

About halfway through that first workday, my crew boss came by to inspect the quality of my work. It turned out that most of the trees I'd planted were not plugged deeply enough into the shallow soil, so I had to replant these initial seedlings, about four hundred, plus an additional four hundred to finish the job.

Despite the setback, I focused on increasing my numbers without sacrificing quality. In order to learn how to plant trees faster and better, I asked one of the most seasoned workers in the crew for some tips, and after incorporating his suggestions, my skills steadily improved with each passing day.

It only took a few days for the crew to finish planting our first location. From there, we moved into an area where the ground had been shaped into mounds of soil by grooming machines, making it ideal for planting.

This contract lasted another few days, and then we were off again. We left Ontario, drove straight through Manitoba, and landed inside the northeastern border of Saskatchewan.

Meanwhile, my numbers kept increasing. By the time we reached our second location in Saskatchewan, I was planting sixteen hundred seedlings per day, a benchmark number that few beginners hit during their first season. Any doubts that I wouldn't make the cut for the summer planting season closed with each passing day. Then, unbelievably, I was accused of cheating, over-claiming the amount of trees I was planting.

It was no secret that there was an increasing discrepancy between the overall numbers claimed by the entire crew and the actual number of trees that were being distributed by the crew bosses. Although we were told that a certain amount of incongruity was normal, for several days prior to the accusation, the supervisor had been warning everyone that the situation was getting out of control, and that people were going to be fired if the cheating didn't slow down.

There were two crews, each comprised of twenty people and overseen by a crew boss. On the same day I got accused, a girl from the other crew was too, each of us singled out by our respective bosses.

Right away I knew why my boss had targeted me. I also knew he was mistaken. He had based his allegations on an inaccurate perception from the day before.

By this time in the season I was carrying four hundred seedlings at a time, the maximum number I could fit into my tree planting bags. I filled my bags at least four times a day, making sixteen hundred the minimum number of trees I was planting each day.

I had reached this plateau a week before, and depending on the length of the workday, could exceed this average by two hundred trees or more. In order to keep my productivity high, I rarely took any breaks throughout the day. But on the day in question, I decided to take it easy.

I had been working in a boggy swamp for the previous few days, and it hardly stopped raining all day. To keep my morale high, I allowed myself a short, ten-minute break each time I returned to reload my bags. By sheer coincidence, my crew boss happened to drive by on one of the company ATVs every time I sat down to rest. I could even tell by the way he kept looking at me what he was thinking.

When the supervisor informed me that I was being fired, I knew my crew boss had assumed I was sitting most of the day and decided that there was no way I could have planted the sixteen hundred trees I recorded that day. Had he taken the time to do an inventory of my planting area he would have realized his mistake before making this rash accusation. But, unfortunately for both of us, he didn't feel the need to do so.

I wanted to be tested emotionally while tree planting, and getting wrongfully accused was certainly a challenge in this regard. I remained calm for the most part, and kept my composure intact, but I was fully determined to clear my name.

Knowing I was innocent, I refused to leave camp until an inventory of any of the areas I had planted was taken. If any of my numbers were off, I agreed to leave, but otherwise, I asserted, the company had no right to fire me.

I doubt whether anyone had ever disputed an accusation before because the supervisor didn't quite know how to deal with the situation.

The following day I wasn't permitted to work, but it was agreed that after the workday was over, my crew boss and I would travel to the location of the last area I had planted and count my trees together.

So, I spent that day at the bush camp, along with the girl from the other crew, whose fate had somehow been bound up with the outcome of mine. Her boyfriend had also taken the day off to console her.

The girl was distressed over the accusation and about the prospect of having to explain what had happened to her family and friends if she was sent home. Her parents had helped finance the necessary investment to work as a tree planter, which required several expensive purchases: steel-toed boots, planting bags, and a shovel, plus all the camping equipment needed to live in the bush.

All day long my concern for this girl grew. As the hours wore on, the three of us chatted to pass the time, but what I really wanted was for this girl to experience the freedom and peace of her true nature. In order for that to happen, I knew I'd need to devise a way to get her to quiet her mind. So, at one point during the day, I suggested the three of us go for a walk on the beach of a nearby lake, thinking that the sound of the waves lapping on the shore might settle her emotions and still her thoughts.

As we were walking along the beach, we came across a huge anthill that was about the same size as a freshly buried human grave. I had just finished eating an apple at the time and placed the core close to the entry point of the colony, hoping the ants devouring it would distract the girl from her distress, at least for a short while.

Thousands of ants covered the apple core in a feeding frenzy, as anticipated. But this activity was soon replaced by a much bigger distraction.

A strange turbulent wind began blowing through a stand of trees lining the upper edge of the beach. The trees started swaying erratically even though the skies were clear.

We all grew a little concerned.

The girl's boyfriend and I both stared at the twisting tree-tops, waiting to see what would happen next. Meanwhile, the girl started walking backwards, instinctively distancing herself from the powerful forces that were gathering overhead.

Yet, as if it was determined to get this girl, the furiously swirling winds swooped down from the treetops and landed right beside her, forming a visible mini-tornado by stirring up the sand on the beach. Then, it bounced off the ground and landed once more, this time directly on top of where she was standing, confining her in a spinning vortex made of sand.

Incredibly, this tiny cyclone swirled around her for a few seconds before lifting off the ground once more and touching down again on the surface of the water. It made a loud gyrating sound like a turbine engine as it whizzed across the lake, creating a funnel-shaped waterspout that sprayed water high into the sky before exhausting itself in the middle of the lake.

A few seconds later, a sprinkling from the ejected water came down, showering us like a burst of rain.

I jumped up ecstatically as soon as it was over and ran straight towards the girl, eager to get her reaction. I looked into her eyes and exclaimed, "That was incredible. You have to tell me what it was like while you were in the center of the cyclone!"

She was mildly in shock, and her eyes looked blank, as if she had just been hypnotized. Finally, after searching to find the right words, she replied, "Perfectly silent."

I reassured her that I was positive everything would be okay. Deep inside I knew that what had just happened was a blessing and a good omen.

My next thought was that I had shamanically summoned this tornado, but the rational side of my brain quickly dismissed the connection as the product of magical thinking, and I put the whole notion out of my head.

Years later, however, when I began experimenting with the power of manifesting by successfully testing if intentions can affect the weather, I would look back at this event as one of the first tangible experiences following my awakening as confirmation that it was actually possible.

I spent the rest of that afternoon mostly alone, waiting for my crew boss to return so that we could take an inventory of my trees. We ended up driving almost two hours to get to the location and then spent another hour and a half counting.

He kept skipping rows and sections, stalling and counting slowly, and even changing the count as we went along, all in the hopes of avoiding what I'm certain he already knew was true.

We got about halfway through the site before it was too dark to continue, but the proof of my innocence was obvious enough even without a final count. A quick survey of the land and a guesstimate of the remaining uncounted seedlings in the field made it look more like I had under-claimed rather than over-claimed.

I tried reasoning with my crew boss, but he was unwilling to listen. It was clear that there were at least sixteen hundred trees planted in that particular plot of land, and I assured him that all my numbers claimed and recorded were also accurate. I even tried explaining to him how he'd made an incorrect correlation between what he thought he saw and what had really happened the day before, but he wouldn't hear any of it. He was absolutely unwilling to admit that he may have made a mistake. So, we were forced to return to base camp with the matter still left unsettled.

It was late at night by the time we got back. My crew boss and I ended up talking with the supervisor in one of the company vans for nearly two hours. But no matter what I said, he was unwilling to admit to possibly making a false and rash accusation. We went around in circles until he mentioned he thought I didn't like him, at which point, the supervisor said he'd heard enough, and that the matter was resolved if we were both willing to leave it alone.

I agreed as long as I could keep my job. I didn't feel the need to force an admission of guilt. However, the resolution to put it behind us was not good enough for my crew boss. He actually insisted that I had to apologize to him for making him feel like I didn't like him. As absurd as it was, I agreed to this request in order to restore peace and harmony.

I was also willing to say sorry because I realized that my impersonality, which is a quality of being that emerges after self-realization, could have been at the heart of what made my crew boss say I didn't like him. It was an important lesson and a powerful reminder to practice being more personable with people in the future.

It was after midnight by the time we ended the meeting. I was still wide awake so I decided to walk down to the beach and do some stargazing before going to bed.

While looking up at the stars, I noticed a thin layer of pale green clouds off in the distance. I didn't pay much attention to them at first. Instead, I used my time alone to relax into the feeling of awe that naturally arises while contemplating the majesty of the starry night sky. But then, a few minutes later, I noticed that the nebula was glowing intensely green.

I'd never seen the aurora borealis before, but once these unusual looking clouds began waving about like curtains, it didn't take me long to figure out that I was viewing the electrically charged particles in the upper atmosphere also known as the northern lights.

For the next five minutes or so, I watched in wonderment as these brilliant phosphorescent particles of energy lit up the entire night sky, blown around in dancing waves by the invisible solar wind.

At first, they were exclusively green, but vibrant tones of red, yellow, and orange emerged, followed by dazzling hues of violet and blue. Soon, it seemed as though every band of color in the visible spectrum of light was weaving itself into this prismatic tapestry.

It was a spectacular display, but what happened next was unbelievable. These huge, multi-hued curtains of light slowly transformed into another vortex. Even more remarkable was its similarity to the one I'd seen on the night of my awakening just before plunging into the Void.

It was a near replica, replete with similar lines of glowing symmetry. The only difference was that instead of feeling like I was standing at the edge of an existential black hole, it felt more like I was beneath a cosmic opening that was funneling nirvanic energies down into this samsaric world of form.

I was open to any messages communicated through this supernatural phenomenon in the same way that I knew that the appearance of the mini-tornado earlier that day was not a coincidence. In other words, I sensed that this spectacle was more than a natural pattern of light and energy. Of course, the rational side of my brain knew there was probably a scientific explanation for this unique formation of the northern lights, but the knowing in my soul recognized the deeper meaning of this event.

In addition to appreciating the significance of seeing yet another vortex, I got the distinct impression that all the karma that had transpired on the ground over the past twenty-four hours was being neutralized or erased by the invisible action of spiritual energies coming down from a higher dimension that was simultaneously materializing this natural event.

When I returned to work the following day, I made a deliberate effort to befriend my crew boss. As a way to heal our relationship, I told him a funny story about a time I kicked an annoying hitchhiker out of my car. He enjoyed the story and our relationship improved from that day forward.

As for the fate of the girl, she was told she could keep her job if she wanted to, which she did.

Several people in the crew still wanted to know what had happened between my crew boss and me, but not wanting to cast negative aspersions on his character, I chose to remain silent and let my return to work speak for itself.

Everyone was watching my performance for proof of my guilt or innocence. If my numbers stayed the same or went up, I would be declared innocent. But if they went down, I would be considered guilty.

In my heart, I knew I was innocent, so I wasn't too concerned with whatever judgment anyone else in the crew had or would eventually pass on me. Plus, a group of my closest workmates and several companions pleaded the case for my innocence to all three bosses the day before, which made me feel good.

However, just to set the official record straight, I wanted the company records to show a significant rise in my planting numbers on that first day back and from then on. I knew that according to the trends used to gauge progress, it would have been regarded as nearly impossible for me to make any sort of significant jump in performance if I had been cheating. So, I set my sites on planting at least two thousand trees that day, a benchmark number reserved for second-year planters.

At this point in the season, my body functioned like a perfectly synchronized machine, each action a coordinated part of a repeatable pattern made to maximize efficiency. I worked nonstop for the entire eight hours.

About half an hour before the workday was officially over, several of the other planters in the area had gathered around my site to watch me work. They periodically asked me for an update of my numbers and called out the remaining time left.

While several of my closest supporters rallied me on with cheers, I blasted through one final row to finish planting the field I was working in just as quitting time approached. The final count: 2147 trees.

After everyone in the crew had assembled at the pick-up location, one of my co-workers, the same person who helped me hone my skills at the beginning of the season, asked me how many trees I had planted. His question came across like a judge's in a courtroom asking the jury if a verdict had been reached, and my response amounted to the last piece of evidence needed before my peers decided if I was guilty or not.

I willingly but humbly shared this bit of information just to clear my name. Someone in the group who was not completely in tune with the ad hoc form of justice taking place asked my intercessor what my answer meant. He replied, loud enough so that everyone could hear, "It means the crew boss made a mistake."

Sensing Meditation
This practice is about being aware of what you are doing while sensing your bodily sensations as fully as possible. Right now it is the awareness of holding this book in your hands, feeling the chair you're sitting on, possibly noticing the sun's warmth on your skin or a breeze blowing into the room, and so on. The same practice of sensing can be done while performing just about any activity: washing dishes, folding laundry, waiting in line, eating a meal, or going for a walk are all opportunities to bring more awareness into your life. By using everyday activities as meditation moments, you'll build a solid foundation for the true nature of your soul to grow stronger and more stable.

Chapter 20

A Synchronistic Encounter with a Pilgrim

THE NEXT DAY, we had a short break. About once a week the company drove us to a local town to take a day or two off from working in the bush. That week we stayed in Yorkton, a city located in southeastern Saskatchewan.

I had spent the first part of the day exploring the town alone, using my time away from the rest of the crew to re-establish the inner peace of my true nature, which had been temporarily disrupted by all the work-related drama.

On my walk, I came across a movie theater and bought a ticket without even bothering to see what was playing. From outside, the building appeared typically plain and utilitarian, but inside it was like stepping back in time to a 1950s-style cinema, which evoked a welcomed feeling of simpler, more carefree times.

Surprisingly, the theatre turned out to be the venue for a short-film festival, and that day they were screening a series of four episodes of *Hammy Hamster's Adventures on the Riverbank*, a Canadian children's television show that I used to love watching as a child, adding a personal memory to the already nostalgic mood of the place.

Halfway through the first episode, I decided to make use of the opportunity to clear my head by dropping into the untroubled wideness of witnessing. I slowly sank back into an open-eyed meditative state and disengaged from the shifting images on the screen. In their place, scenes from the drama at work began projecting themselves onto the inner screen of my mind, which I watched pass by with the same disinterest I had towards the images emerging from the movie projector.

By the time the closing credits for the last episode were rolling, all the scenes from the situation at work had stopped surfacing in my mind, allowing me to move forward in peace and leave behind any lingering feelings about what had happened.

After leaving the theater, I made my way over to a local laundromat, which was one of the designated pick-up spots for the return drive back to camp. Several friends from my crew were already there, waiting. At some point, a few of us gathered outside and started discussing what we were going to do with the money we were making from tree planting. I mentioned maybe buying a motorcycle and traveling before returning home.

I had ridden motorcycles throughout my teenage years and always dreamt of touring the countryside this way. It wasn't something I set my heart on doing, but I was open to the idea of making it happen, if I earned enough dough.

I had just finished sharing my potential traveling plans when someone riding a motorcycle with a "For Sale" sign pulled up outside the laundromat. Once again, I knew it was more than a coincidence. I had experienced this phenomenon before, although I didn't know what it was called yet.

Carl Jung first described it in the 1920s, which he called *synchronicity*. And more recently, James Redfield, author of the popular novel *The Celestine Prophecy*, narrated how synchronicity can lead us forward on the path of personal and collective spiritual evolution.

I approached the rider, introduced myself, and learned that his name was Tim. I explained that I was working in the bush as a tree planter and was thinking about buying a bike so I could do a bit of exploring and traveling on my way back home.

Tim told me he was originally from Peterborough, not too far from my hometown in Toronto, and had ridden the bike from there. We briefly discussed the possibility of me buying his motorcycle, but the conversation quickly shifted gears, so to speak.

After briefly mentioning the serendipity of his arrival, Tim gathered that I'd experienced a spiritual awakening and invited me indoors to continue talking.

I have no idea how long we talked. All I remember is that it was dark outside when the van back to base camp pulled up. It was time to leave just when it felt like we were getting started. So, I asked Tim if we could meet again in a week.

I knew that the company would be returning to Yorkton one more time before moving on to the next work site, so Tim and I made plans to reconnect on my next day off, seven days later. As a parting gift, Tim loaned me the only existing copy of a manuscript he had written and illustrated. He described it as a fictional story about a wandering homeless man, adding that the inspiration for the book came from his spiritual journey.

During the intervening week, I kept trying to read Tim's manuscript. I knew that there was a deeper spiritual message below the surface of the story, but I just couldn't get into the receptive frame of mind that was required. And tree planting, especially that week, provided almost zero opportunities to read quietly and reflect.

Since the bush camp was far from the planting site, there was a daily commute to and from work, and I've never been able to read in a moving vehicle. Breakfast and dinner were served at a restaurant that was an additional hour out of the way, so we had to get up extra early and arrived home quite late every day due to the extended commute. And finally, that week we had to travel deep into the bush over muddy logging roads on the flatbed of a slow-moving tracked vehicle, and the noise and smell of the gurgling diesel engine, along with the crowded conditions and bumpy ride, made it totally impossible to read. So, as much as I tried to make it happen, a deep reading of Tim's manuscript just wasn't meant to be.

I returned to Yorkton a week later and met Tim at the coffee shop as planned. After we finished eating lunch, Tim invited me to his apartment so we could continue talking more privately. On our way there, he asked me if I'd read his manuscript. I apologized and explained that as much as I wanted to, I was only able to skim over it, so he suggested we find a place to photocopy the book so that I could take it with me.

With Tim at the coffee shop

We spent the next hour searching around town before we were eventually forced to abandon the project. It was a Sunday and the only place that was open wanted to charge an unreasonable amount of money for the job. Although it ended up curtailing the amount of time we would otherwise have spent at Tim's apartment talking, the remaining time we had together was more than enough for the purpose of our meeting, which by this time we both realized was not really about exchanging anything tangible like a motorcycle or a book.

Tim worked for a local plumber, his profession by trade, and was renting an apartment from the owner above the shop. It was a small room, just barely big enough for one person. It housed a single spring cot along the back wall and a kitchenette with a small table. We sat at the kitchen table and talked for close to an hour.

During our limited time together, Tim and I spoke about many things that helped me understand and validate my awakening. At the start of our conversation, he asked me to describe my experience of enlightenment. I explained how I had descended into a vortex of infinite regression and contraction. Beyond that pithy phrase, I had few other words or concepts to describe what had occurred on the night of my awakening. But Tim looked at me knowingly, and remarkably to me at the time, he understood what I meant.

During another pivotal point in our conversation, Tim took out a piece of paper and said that he was going to draw a symbol for me that he knew I would find very meaningful. He asked me to close my eyes while he drew it. When he was finished he placed it on the table in front of me.

I opened my eyes and looked down at a square piece of white paper about two inches wide. Tim had folded it twice, neatly in half both times, creating four quartered sections. I knew what he had drawn even before looking at it. I opened the paper and saw the image I had anticipated. It was an X. But Tim had also drawn a circle around it, which was an unexpected addition.

This simple diagram captured my understanding of the spiritual path in a deeply symbolic way. Without being able to explain it in words, I knew that the circle represented the paradoxical fullness and emptiness of the formless dimension, and in combination with the X, created a slightly more complex pattern that symbolized the path to enlightenment.

The lower half of the X is like an arrow pointing upwards, representing the spiritual aspiration to reach the higher plane of consciousness, while the top half represents the expansion of consciousness that occurs after enlightenment is reached.

Tim asked for my response to the symbol, but all I could share was that I had encountered the same symbol minus the circle as a subtle form in my consciousness, and that it was instrumental in catalyzing the transformation I underwent on the night of my awakening.

Tim knowingly confirmed the authenticity of my awakening with another wordless gaze. Then, after sharing this non-verbal exchange, he added that I was one of the *chosen ones*.

Now, I know what you're thinking. It sounded messianic to me, too. But Tim went on to explain that it only meant that I was going to help others awaken their true nature, which I could accept without it becoming the kind of spiritual ego trap that leads to a superiority complex.

We parted company soon after this. As a farewell gift, Tim gave me the original cover of his illustrated manuscript as a memento of our encounter, which I've kept as a reminder of the kind of supernatural aid that often appears on the spiritual path.

Chapter 21

Working in the World

A FTER RETURNING HOME from my tree planting adventure, I began looking for new job opportunities. Once again, I focused on finding work that would assist the process of stabilizing my true nature. Having always enjoyed physical work and being outdoors, I applied for a job as a letter carrier with Canada Post, again for many of the same reasons I sought out work in tree planting.

I successfully made it through the first two stages of the hiring process and only needed to show up for a final interview to assess if I had the right kind of personality for the job. That interview was scheduled for Monday morning the following week.

On the preceding Thursday, I learned of another employment prospect. This job posting came from an organization in Waterloo, Ontario, called The Network, whose mandate was to help advance the field of mediation in Canada.

Shortly after my awakening, I started volunteering as a community mediator at St. Stephen's Community House, a social service agency in Toronto. It was because of my work there that I received the job posting from The Network.

I immediately contacted the project coordinator, Kathleen, and expressed my enthusiasm for the position over the phone. After explaining that I was about to be hired for a new job the following Monday, I requested an early interview, which she agreed to give me the next day, a Friday.

The project was designed to give fifteen young people an opportunity to deliver conflict resolution workshops to various organizations in the community. Fortunately, I was hired for one of the fifteen available spots. One of the highlights of the project was the freedom to be creative. Dance, music, art, and drama were specifically encouraged as teaching methods.

Another unique aspect of this project was learning how to work as part of a team using a combination of aboriginal healing circle and group facilitation skills. We were put into teams of three, dubbed *small circles*, and met daily with the group, or *main circle*, which was made up of all five teams.

Each day began with a main circle meeting to share ideas and information, debrief work-related experiences, and facilitate effective planning and execution of the day-to-day business tasks. Emphasis was placed on creating an atmosphere that valued cooperation, open communication, and consensus building, while also fostering positive self-esteem and peer support among participants.

Every Friday morning, we engaged in group activities to promote team building and leadership, and in the afternoon we met with numerous guest speakers whose methodology we could implement in our social work in the community.

It was a wonderful time filled with amazing opportunities that contributed to my development as a community leader as well as a spiritual teacher. The next six months was essentially a crash course in catalyzing the power of the human spirit to create positive changes in the world.

The following story epitomizes the transformational nature of this project.

It happened one night at a shelter for women where I was co-facilitating a support group with Scott and Rachel, the two other members in our smaller team of three. One of the initial challenges we had to overcome was getting permission to enter Mary's Place, the name of the shelter. It was run by the YWCA, the largest women's organization in the world.

To ensure that Mary's Place remained a haven of safety and refuge for women, men were forbidden from entering the premises without explicit permission, and only then on rare occasions. As far as men running any sort of programming, the YWCA had a strict mandate to provide female-centered programming in female-only venues.

Since two of us were males, we had to discover a way to convince the Programming Director of the YWCA to make an exception. During a brainstorming session, Scott suggested serving the women in the cafeteria during dinnertime on the same night as our support group. This would allow them to interact with positive male role models, as well as give us an opportunity to invite them to participate in our group.

It actually worked. And so, for the first time in its history, Mary's Place allowed two male volunteers to help run a program for the women in the shelter.

The women who showed up varied in age and faced a variety of painful life predicaments and difficult challenges. We developed a simple process to explore the possibility of creating change in the women's lives. To foster peer support and open sharing among participants, we incorporated the principles and practices used in aboriginal healing circles, and used a form of drama therapy taught to us by Kathleen, the visionary leader of this project.

We ran our program on Wednesday nights. The first two meetings went reasonably well, but on the third night something extraordinary happened. A distinct shift occurred in the group's energy during a warm-up exercise we were doing.

It was a simple activity that involved pairing up with a partner and sharing a personal story. Suddenly, for no apparent reason, a powerful force of healing energy descended on the group. The energy was quite tangible as it moved through the room. As this was happening, one of the older women in the group mentioned something miraculous was occurring.

A young woman suffering from a borderline personality disorder suddenly jumped up and began recreating a scene from her childhood that demonstrated how her mother lacked warmth. Then, a mostly despondent elderly woman who had been living at Mary's Place for years, volunteered to help this young woman work through her unresolved emotions. The elderly woman began role-playing the younger woman's mother, substituting in the present moment the maternal love she had not received growing up.

While this was going on, two other women in the group who had been in a bitter and brutal fight earlier in the week each asked the other to be forgiven for any wrongdoing. They exchanged sobbing words of confession and openly embraced while the rest of the women in the group surrounded them and offered emotional support and containment.

After this breakthrough, the energy settled down, and the rest of the evening was spent debriefing and giving thanks for the remarkable series of events that had unfolded. But what was so much more amazing is that the waves of healing had a ripple effect beyond the circle we ran that night.

The following week the project coordinator of the YWCA reported that the rate of violence in the shelter had dropped significantly since our last session. The police, who were normally called to settle a dispute as often as two or three times a week, weren't phoned once during the entire week, and this peaceful effect continued unabated for weeks thereafter.

The project was only funded for six months. However, because it was so successful, the funding was renewed so that the project could be duplicated. This second time around I was hired, along with another participant, Glenn, to run the project. It was another amazing learning opportunity, with too many transformational stories to recount here.

After this project ended, I was asked to run it again, but I decided to return to university to finish my degree instead. However, before returning to school, I worked on one more project with The Network. Developing a peace and conflict resolution curriculum for the Colombian schooling system. I was hired to work on the first phase of the project, which took place in Cartagena.

My official role was to represent the youth and share my perspectives with teachers and educators. At the beginning of the conference, I was asked to stand up and speak to the assembly. This was not discussed prior to that moment, so I was taken a bit off guard, especially since I wasn't comfortable speaking in public yet.

As I walked up to the podium, however, a vast calmness came over me, and I began to see the sequence of relevant experiences working in this field.

I spoke briefly about one of my high school teachers encouraging me to become a peer mediator, and how I went on to work as a community mediator for St. Stephen's and was then hired first as a project participant and then as a youth leader for The Network.

I also related how the communication skills I had learned from the conflict resolution and mediation training I received during high school came at a crucial time in my life, helping me to get along better with my girlfriend, as well as with my family and friends.

The speech was well received, yet the whole time I was speaking, what I really wanted to share was my understanding of enlightenment. I knew it wasn't the right time or place to share this information with others, though.

Later that night, while lying in bed, thinking about the deeper purpose of my life, I had a vision. A flaming blue, luminous Buddha appeared in my mind's eye, which I took as a positive sign that I was meant to guide others on the path to enlightenment.

After the conference ended, I extended the return date of my ticket by four days so that I could go on a personal retreat before returning to Canada. Some friends helped set me up at a rustic resort on a tiny island off the coast of Cartagena. I was the only guest staying there at the time. It was perfect.

In my heart, I knew that I had to figure out a way to tell others about enlightenment, so I started writing again. I began with what I would have said at the conference if I'd been asked to speak about the pursuit of peace and the practices of conflict resolution from a spiritual perspective. Not exactly what I wanted to express, but it was a starting point.

I spent the next four days sitting at a table outside in the open sun, waiting for the inspiration to write. At times, the words and ideas flowed together, and at other times, I just sat in silence, staring off into space, resting in the simple freedom of enlightened awareness.

Four days later, I had several pages filled with some of my ideas about the importance of witnessing as a conflict resolution practice. I described how this impersonal observer can help us detach from our thoughts and feelings during a conflict to avoid reacting, and how this same level of awareness can be used to see these situations objectively and deal with them more wisely and effectively.

I returned home and continued working on this project, the first writing I started since my awakening. I had originally thought of writing some sort of practical manual for mediators and practitioners in the field of conflict resolution, but I gradually moved away from a specific goal and allowed my writing to become a field of exploration without predetermining the direction or overall shape of the work. I continued to add material to this project whenever I could.

Years later, I eventually wrote a book entitled *Heaven On Earth: A Guide to Enlightenment & Human Unity* that was culled together from the voluminous pages I had amassed. Although I didn't feel ready to write my autobiography yet, a few days before *Heaven On Earth* was going to be printed, I pulled it off the press because I felt strongly that something important was missing.

Knowing that part of fulfilling my destiny involved telling others about my awakening, I wrote an autobiographical sketch that I included as a Preface. Then, when I finally felt ready to share the story of my spiritual journey, I expanded upon that brief account until it evolved into this book.

After returning home from Colombia, I went back to university and finished my degree as planned. Following that, I was lucky enough to get a job as a supply teacher, which was an excellent way to support myself financially while making progress spiritually.

This job strengthened my group leadership and teaching skills, which I knew would be useful in my future role as a spiritual teacher. And it also allowed me to take time off work whenever I felt the need to focus on my writing.

The demand for supply teachers was so high at the time that I got to work with students at every grade level in both elementary and high school, learning to relate to children and adolescents of all ages, which I really enjoyed.

Then, in a strange twist of fate, I ended up being hired to work exclusively with students with special needs, which led to the development of certain non-ordinary abilities.

Amazing things happened when working with students with autism. I discovered I could psychically tune into their muted interior world and then draw them out.

This resulted in improved verbal communication, reduction of repetitive behaviors, increased interest in constructive activities, and more socializing and emotional bonding, which are all areas of development where people with autism tend to exhibit resistance or impairment.

Several colleagues asked me how I was able to relate and work so well with these students in particular, but I had no way of openly sharing or explaining the real reasons for my success, which was based on an intuitive sense that there are four main centers in every human being.

The first is the belly center, which is connected with being grounded in the body and in reality. The second is the heart center, which has to do with feeling the full range of human emotions necessary for relating and connecting with others. The third is the head center, which supplies the intelligence needed for understanding life. And the fourth is the higher self center, which is located above the head and connects our consciousness to the formless dimension.

In my experience, people with autism mostly inhabit the head and overhead centers, with less presence or activity in the heart and belly centers. By magnifying my own presence in these lower centers, I was able to get them to do the same.

I also had a lot of success working with students with behavior problems, partly due to my conflict resolution training and social work experiences. In one class I worked in, comprised of fifteen special needs students who all had behavior problems, learning disabilities, and various degrees of attention deficit hyperactivity disorder, I secretly and playfully introduced meditation at the start of each class by calling it the *stillness challenge.* Meditating with my students significantly improved their concentration and lessened hyperactivity.

In sum, being a schoolteacher was a wonderful learning opportunity, and on a personal level, I found the work deeply gratifying. In one last unexpected blessing, I ended up teaching at my old high school, and during that time, several colleagues, many of whom had been my teachers, made a point of telling me not to quit teaching as a career path, explaining that they felt I belonged in a classroom and that I could go as far as I wanted to in the education system.

I'm not sure how true it was, but it certainly felt good to hear. Yet, as encouraging as their words were, I knew that my true calling lay in a different type of teaching.

Chapter 22

The Journey of Descent

I REMAINED IN A TRANSCENDENTAL STATE of awareness for approximately three years following my awakening. Once I was certain that the connection to my higher self had become a permanent adaptation, I felt inwardly drawn to embark on the journey of descent. Part of my decision to do so was to get re-embodied, but I was also motivated to take on extra spiritual work, which I'll explain at the end of this chapter.

As usual, I followed the intuitive promptings guiding me throughout my life, so when the impulse to descend emerged, I trusted it was something I had to do, even though I wasn't sure why at the time. In hindsight, I do now. The completion of the spiritual journey isn't found in a transcendence of the world, although the soul may remain in the higher dimension of formless freedom for a while.

In my case, this transcendental period lasted about three years, though for others it may last as long as thirty years, or as short as three weeks, three days, three minutes, or sometimes even just a few seconds. Yet, no matter the duration of one's transcendental sojourn, at some point, the journey of descent ensues, which, more often than not, usually happens involuntarily.

In fact, for the majority of seekers, the path to enlightenment is normally characterized by a series of glimpses of the higher self, which gradually leads to a permanent change in consciousness over time. In Zen Buddhism, for example, such glimpses are called *kensho*, while the term for a more lasting awakening is *satori*, with full self-realization often described as many kenshos leading to satori.

At the same time, some seekers awaken without any peak experiences. This is possible because we already are the timeless presence we seek (although we're usually unaware of it), but if primed to penetrate this paradox of enlightenment, the necessary inner shift is like traveling to a place one never left.

Back to my journey, and more specifically, the journey of descent as I experienced it, because I wasn't sure about the outcome of this movement beforehand, I actually resisted coming down from the transcendental summit of consciousness. I was worried about losing the feeling of bliss and freedom from abiding in my higher self. I was so concerned about this possibility, in fact, that I ended up waiting several months before tackling this endeavor.

A comment made during a conversation marked the moment I decided to follow through with this decision. I was on my way home one night with an old friend of the family, a Cree Indian man from Saskatchewan who we affectionately call Big Bear. Out of the blue, he turned to me and casually asked, "So, what's it like up there?"

We had never spoken about what had happened to me, yet I wasn't overly surprised that he could sense I was living in a transcendental state of being. I also knew that his comment was not a coincidence. On a deeper level of knowing, I knew that his soul was speaking directly to mine, signaling that it was time for me to make the descent that I'd been contemplating embarking on.

Mildly shocked but also pleasantly surprised, I jokingly answered, "It's kind of lonely. I'm thinking about joining the rest of you down there at the base of the mountain!"

He chuckled at my comment, but even though I made it humorously, the moment I said it, I knew it was time to take the plunge. Then and there, I asked God to make it happen. The next morning I awoke knowing the process of descending had begun.

For years, I had been orbiting above my head in the freedom of higher consciousness, and the sensation of leaving that liberated position and re-entering the denser atmosphere of physical reality was quite palpable. It felt like sinking into quicksand.

Later on that day, an important sign appeared in a synchronistic way. I was an active follower of a now defunct web forum dedicated to the work of Ken Wilber, an American philosopher who writes about enlightenment and is best known for his **Integral Theory.**

On the same day that I was descending, a member began posting multiple lines made solely of V's that were arranged in such a way that columns of these repeating letters waved from side to side as you scrolled down the screen. I instantly saw their significance. Not only did the V's match the upper half of the X that had facilitated my awakening in 1996, but the pattern created by this post captured the sensation I felt as my consciousness spiraled down from above that day.

The paradoxical nature of this person's contribution to the dialogue caused some intrigue in the online community, and although I didn't offer any comments on the apparent randomness of the post, it definitely spoke to me in a deeply symbolic way, helping to ease my descent.

By the time I went to bed that night, I had descended so much that I felt submerged below the earth, *literally*. Prior to this descent, the location of my identity was approximately an arm's length above my head, whereas after this descent, it was the same distance from my body, only in the exact opposite direction, placing it a foot and a half below my feet.

For the next few months, I experienced the most dreadful feelings imaginable. My whole being was drenched in sorrow. I felt like I had fallen from the highest heights to a place so low that I couldn't even begin to imagine what it might be like to function in the world as a normal human being again. I was plagued by the thought that I'd made a major spiritual error.

Thankfully, I received another sign during this period. I was driving westbound on a stretch of Ontario Highway 401 near Whitby one day, only to discover thousands of upward pointing V-shaped symbols on the expressway.

They are called chevrons and were painted in each lane as part of a government initiative to reduce tailgating. The significance of this synchronicity was compounded by the fact that this was the first and only time that this particular traffic symbol was used in Ontario. Even more coincidental, the project was discontinued shortly after being introduced, adding another element of congruency between both the appearance and subsequent disappearance of these traffic symbols with the events of my spiritual journey.

Most of the chevrons have since faded, and the signs stating their use removed. At the time, however, these upward pointing symbols meaningfully reflected a mirror image of the downward pointing V's that had appeared previously. It was an undeniable indication of the ascending movement of consciousness that would be required to get re-embodied.

A few days later, I went to a place I often visited in my youth whenever I felt the need to spend time thinking about the deeper purpose of my life. There is a hill across the street where I grew up called Seneca Hill. According to the unconfirmed history of this hill, it was a sacred burial ground for the Seneca people, one of the First Nations groups who lived in the area before European settlement.

A panoramic view of the horizon graces the top of this local summit, which was an ideal place to elicit the expansive states of being that I'd always known were the defining challenge of my life to maintain and ultimately share with others. I sat on top of this hill hoping to gain some indication of how I might climb back up to the transcendental heights of formless freedom again.

The view from Seneca Hill

Desperate but determined, I turned my attention inward while looking upward in search of another sign. Remarkably, a column of consciousness opened up above my head, and running through the center of it was a well-known phenomenon called the *silver cord* in spiritual literature, which is described as a subtle life-giving linkage between the higher self and the physical body, much like the umbilical cord is our lifeline to our mother's body during pregnancy.

As soon as I witnessed the appearance of this luminous thread, I felt certain I'd regain the liberating perspective of my higher self. Even after seeing this spiritual link, however, a lot of striving still remained.

Each day I had to focus my energy on climbing to a higher state of being, raising my consciousness in tiny increments that slowly lifted both my mood and the locus of my soul in tandem.

It took several weeks before the seat of my consciousness was back inside my body. But there was only one problem. I mistakenly believed that I had to keep raising my consciousness above my body and return to the overhead position of abiding in my higher self.

As a result of this error in my thinking, I focused on re-acquiring the freedom of worldly transcendence once again, rather than adapting to becoming an embodied, self-realized human being in the world.

In order to reunite with my higher self, I decided to work with the chakras. The seven most commonly described ones are located in an ascending order from the base of the spine to the top of the head. For the purpose of awakening, there are certain sounds that open each of these chakras, somewhat like climbing a ladder.

The following is a brief description of the vowel sounds associated with all seven chakras. Their locations are shown in the accompanying diagram. If you decide to try chakra chanting, it is important to allow yourself the freedom to play with the sounds to find the ideal modulations for you. We are all unique vibratory beings and the frequency or pitch of each sound, as well as the vowel sounds associated with each chakra, can all be ad-

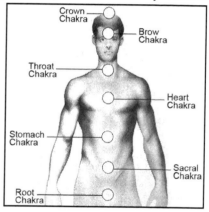

justed. In general, you should find that the deeper tones resonate in the lower chakras, and that the higher tones resonate in the upper chakras.

The vibrational sound for the root chakra is "UHH" and has the same vowel sound as in the word *hut*. The vibrational sound for the sacral chakra is "OOO" and has the same vowel sound as in the word *too*. The vibrational sound for the stomach chakra is "OHH" and is the same sound as the long letter *o*. The vibrational sound for the heart chakra is "AHH"

and is like the sound you make when relaxing into a sooth-
ing bath. The vibrational sound for throat chakra is "EYE"
and is the same sound as the word *eye*. The vibrational sound
for the brow chakra is "AYE" and is the same vowel sound as
in the word *hay*. The vibrational sound for the crown chakra
is "EEE" and is pronounced like the long letter *e*.[3]

Every night, I'd take a warm bath and chant the sounds
associated with each chakra, while focusing the vibrations of
the sounds at their respective locations along the front of my
body. After doing this for about thirty minutes, I'd unplug the
stopper and sink into the formless depths of being as fully as
possible. As an aid, I would use the falling waterline to wash
my bodily identity away until there was nothing left but my
awareness, floating *in* and *as* an ocean of pure consciousness.

I repeated this activity for months. With continued practice, I eventually discovered how to resonate all of the chakras
using a single sweeping tone, opening a central channel in the
body known as the *sushumna*, which connects the root chakra
to the crown chakra. Once activated, the latent kundalini energy stored at the base of the spine rises through the sushumna,
activating each of the chakras on its ascension, bringing us into deeper and more expanded states of being along the way,
until we experience our true nature as boundless beings.

Soon after making this discovery, I experienced another
breakthrough that simultaneously replaced the need to chant
outwardly and course-corrected my attempt to climb back up
to my higher self.

I was lying in the empty tub at the time, after having just
completed my chakra chants. A buzzing sound, similar to the
whiny song of a cicada, began vibrating in my head, and as I
tuned into it, this hum ascended in pitch and morphed into a
higher, more pleasing tone. As this was happening, I ascended

out of my body and merged with my higher self with the same impact that I had experienced in 1996. Right away it occurred to me that my consciousness had already been so fully transformed since then that the connection to my higher self had never actually been lost. In a sudden epiphany, I understood that the purpose for the journey of descent was to ground my awareness in my body, which had already happened.

Subjectively, I went from experiencing myself as this vast window hovering overhead to the same measureless sense of awareness extending outwardly from my body without end. It still feels like a window through which the clear light of nondual awareness shines freely. The only difference is that this same lens of liberation is now located on the ground level.

Although a significant part of my focus at the start of my journey of descent was to get re-embodied, as I mentioned at the beginning of this chapter, I was also motivated by another goal: clearing a pathway through the **collective unconscious** to make enlightenment more available to humanity.

It is important to point out that this is not a usual part of the journey of descent. However, it can become part of one's path if you choose to go beyond your own enlightenment and work towards the enlightenment of the world. I'll reference two contemporary mystics who agree in a moment.

I knew that this endeavor would involve the assimilation of massive amounts of collective karma, but I felt up for the task and motivated to accomplish this goal. This period coincided with the part of my journey when I was below my body, which, to reiterate, is not a normal part of the process of getting re-embodied.

I've already mentioned how badly I felt during this time. Just to elaborate a bit more, during my waking state I was plagued by ancient fears and primitive reactions to life, and countless nights were spent fighting sadistic and tormented beings in recurring nightmarish dreams.

This activity continued until a major shift finally came one night during a far more uplifting dream. As soon as the dream started, I knew it was more than an ordinary dream and that I had actually entered and positively influenced the collective unconscious in some mysterious occult way.

Here, I was bodiless. Only my awareness remained. Beneath me a vast expanse of perfectly symmetrical yellow bricks stretched out forever, and above there was nothing but blue sky and an invisible sun that bronzed the air and gave everything a soft warm glow.

In addition to the vivid colors and immense features in this arcane space, the whole atmosphere had an omniscient quality that made everything feel alive with the heightened clarity of nondual awareness. And finally, my own awareness was spinning like an auger, trying to dig through the endless tract of yellow bricks.

It was immediately apparent that this was a futile effort. The bedrock was impenetrable. The message was clear. The perpetual brickwork symbolized the stony equanimity of witnessing, which, along with the omniscient atmosphere permeating this environment, signaled that I had successfully opened a channel for the liberating energies of enlightenment to descend into the lowest depths of the collective human psyche. Once this was done, I worked on getting re-embodied.

As with all the mystical processes from my life, the experiences usually came first. It was only later, after the fact, that I would do research to put them into context.

In terms of matching the events described above with references in the spiritual literature of the world, several sources document the existence of transpersonal chakras above the head,[4] as well as subpersonal chakras below the feet,[5] which corresponds with my experiences of being situated both over and under my body for distinct periods of my journey.

With respect to facing the collective unconscious, according to the contemporary mystic and spiritual teacher David R. Hawkins, at more advanced stages of spiritual evolution, the overall karmic inheritance of humanity is confronted and transcended.[6] Also, the twentieth-century sage Aurobindo and his collaborator, Mirra Alfassa, described engaging and overcoming negative regions in the collective psyche of humanity as part of their spiritual work.

Finally, the ascending sound wave that I heard during my second experience of enlightenment is documented in many modern and ancient traditions. One of the most well-known sources is Shabd Yoga, but references can also be found in Esoteric Christianity, Sufism, Sikhism, as well as the religious movement Eckankar. It is described in these traditions as an audible sound current that resounds within all humans and the whole of creation. I call it the *Sonic Truth*. Tuning into this frequency is a great way to reconnect with your higher self. The shaded box below explains how to develop the ability to hear and benefit from the expansiveness of this inner sound.

Sonic Truth Meditation
Sitting erect with your eyes closed, listen for a faint ringing sound inside your head. Tune into and keep listening for this subtle inner sound during meditation. As your mind grows quieter, you'll begin to hear it. Once you do, it will resonate more. As it does, the amplifying effect of this tone simultaneously expands your consciousness and acts like a tuning fork that opens the sushumna, which aligns your whole being with your higher self.

Chapter 23

The Union of Marriage

B ACK AT THE START OF MY JOURNEY OF DESCENT, while delaying the return to my body, my brother John gave me a book of transcribed talks by Jiddu Krishnamurti, a renowned writer and speaker on philosophical and spiritual subjects.

My brother asked me if I had ever heard of Krishnamurti and suggested I might enjoy reading one of his books. At the time, I was aware of Krishnamurti by name and had pieced together a few details about his life from my research. I knew of his early association with the Theosophical Society, as well as his radical departure from that spiritual group after he rejected their edification of him as the next Messiah.

I welcomed my brother's gift and began leafing through the book. A passage about marriage immediately grabbed my attention. The questioner asked Krishnamurti if being married was counterproductive to the higher aims of the spiritual path. He answered that a person enjoying the freedom of spiritual liberation should be capable of being in a romantic, loving relationship in an unproblematic way.

I was in a relationship when I went through my transformation, but I eventually ended it and had stayed both single and celibate up until this point in my life. However, as soon as I read this passage, I realized I still felt a deep longing for a spiritual partner, someone to walk and work with on my journey through life. I could have ignored this desire, but I felt it would be beneficial for my ongoing development.

For one thing, I knew that being in a committed relationship with a woman would force my heart and soul to mature in ways that I felt it probably wouldn't have otherwise. I was also reading certain tantric teachings at the time, which stress that sexual union is a useful way to get the energy needed to become a fully embodied, liberated human being. And finally, anticipating my role as a spiritual teacher, I wanted to be able to demonstrate through my own life that it is possible to be happily married and still continue to enjoy life and evolve spiritually without living like an ascetic yogi.

I had a few brief relationships, but for one reason or another, none of them were quite right. So, I eventually decided to manifest a partner. At this stage in my journey, I had successfully experimented with the Law of Attraction, an ability made popular by *The Secret*, a 2006 film about using visualization to manifest what you desire into your life.

At the time, the film hadn't been made yet, but I had already discovered that it was possible to willfully draw things into reality. It was another one of the abilities emerging during this post-awakening period.

Knowing that the power to manifest required the use of mental imagery combined with intention, I began envisioning the personal qualities I felt would make an ideal partner. My main focus was to find someone who would be supportive of the kind of spiritual work I was engaged in.

In addition to sending out these intentions, I called upon the Divine for assistance, trusting that God knew better than me what kind of wife I'd need. So, using the powers of manifestation in combination with prayer, I asked God to find me a spiritual companion.

I was working at Brebeuf College, the same high school I had attended as a student in my youth, when I met Aniko. I had been hired full-time on an extended contract to assist the Special Education department, which was an area of teaching she'd been considering specializing in.

In another interesting parallel, even though Aniko resisted the idea of teaching at an all-boys' school, she had followed a series of synchronistic signs leading up to her internship at Brebeuf that guided her to be there at the same time as me.

On the day we first met, Aniko came into my classroom intending to ask me some questions about Special Education, but for some unknown reason, she later recounted, she felt compelled to ask me about yoga and meditation instead. I had already noticed her arrival at the school days before and knew even before she entered my classroom that she was the one I had been waiting for.

What followed next was a wonderful journey through a variety of new and exciting spiritual experiences that brought the two of us together in a way that was more magical than either of us had ever experienced while falling in love before.

During the first few weeks that we were getting to know each other, we'd meet in the teacher's lounge on our breaks and often went for walks in a nearby ravine after work.

As discrete as we tried to be, it was obvious what was happening. We were so instantly compatible with each other that several colleagues were convinced we knew each other from a previous time in our lives.

Although we repeatedly explained that we'd never met before, secretly, on a deeper level of knowing, we both shared the sense that we'd been together in previous lifetimes.

As hoped for, falling in love with Aniko triggered the forces of both *immanence* and *transcendence* to begin flowing into my being, which, surprisingly, began happening several months before we even became sexually active.

Not only did these energies help ground me back in my body, the co-mingling of these forces also generated a tacit feeling that made our coming together reaffirm the true nature of reality as a union of the formless dimension and the world of form. What's more, this experience helped reintegrate and infuse the absolute truth back into the very essence of my be-ing in a spiritually grounded and embodied way.

The fusion of these energies also created an energy field that we both felt and perceived surrounding us. This shared aura manifested as a subtly perceptible and felt energetic bub-ble that formed whenever we were in each other's company. No matter where we were, the moment we got together, this energetic bubble would envelop us, and inside it was just the two of us, experiencing each other as the most wonderful be-ing we'd ever met.

Then, even more remarkably, an opening appeared at the top of our bubble one day, and like curious children looking down a wishing well, I saw several luminous beings hover-ing above us, their ephemeral forms scintillating as if made of the finest filaments of spiritual light.

It was quite clear to me that they had intentionally gath-ered overhead to open this huge vortex, which functioned like a portal connecting their luminous world to ours. There were hundreds of these ethereal beings hanging about in the inter-dimensional space above our heads, and I could hear the re-joicing laughter of those who were closest.

Aniko didn't perceive them as plainly as I did, but their shared excitement was still very tangible, which we both felt showering down on us as waves of loving energy. That we were both sensing the presence of these visitors surprised us at first, but since we'd recently shared how each of us had visualized and prayed for a suitable partner at this stage in our lives, we deduced that they must have been instrumental in helping us find each other.

In fact, I got the impression that this gathering was made up of **angels**, **spirit guides**, and **soul companions**, all of whom had worked together to ensure that Aniko and I found each other. I even sensed that they wanted me to recognize that we had received their help by showing themselves and providing a glimpse of the spirit world.

Once it seemed as though all these luminous beings had a good look, they slowly receded from the opening above us, and we never saw them again. Over the next few years, Aniko and I began building a life together. Then, in 2005, we eloped to Australia, where we exchanged our wedding vows on a riverbank in Melbourne.

Chapter 24

Bringing Light Down into the World

THE MOST INSPIRING REVELATION I received during the transformation I underwent in 1996 is that humanity is on the verge of undergoing a collective awakening. Since then, with the rising number of people around the world going through intense personal changes and spiritual transformations, I'm convinced that this process is already underway.

Also, according to predictions made by the ancient Hindu, Egyptian, and Mayan civilizations, we have already entered a new era of accelerated spiritual development and increased global harmony, the effects of which, I believe, can be seen in the emergence of the internet, the environmental movement, and the growth of social activism around the globe, to give a few examples.

On my thirty-third birthday, soon after I began teaching in public, I experienced another revelation that deepened my understanding of the actual nature of a collective awakening. As part of this same mystical experience, a process was set in motion that culminated in my ability to bring spiritual light and other divine energies down into the world, in large part, to help assist this shift.

I'd been hoping to acquire this ability prior to its arrival, so this development didn't come as a huge surprise, but the mystical experience that brought it about was a bit shocking. In fact, this experience was so different from anything else I'd ever experienced before that I had to accept certain **New Age** teachings to validate what had transpired – something I wasn't inclined to do previously.

I was at home when the breakthrough occurred.

Aniko and I had spent the morning talking about our life together, looking back at the year in review and setting goals and intentions for the next year and beyond. After finishing our conversation, she went upstairs to do some work on her computer, while I remained alone in the living room to reflect some more.

It was drizzling and foggy that day, which is the perfect weather to appreciate the nondual mystery of existence. So, I decided to drop into witnessing to elicit and appreciate the oneness of everything.

I was standing in front of our living room window at the time, watching a steady stream of morning commuter traffic drift by. Sure enough, the nondual nature of reality began to shine forth with typical crystal clarity, which was a familiar experience for me. However, there was an unusual intensity infusing this immaculate perception. Everything was throbbing with life, including me. My whole being was expanding and contracting in unison with the subtle pulses of formless energy that I could both see and feel were manifesting reality into existence.

Then, even more strikingly, a beam of golden light shone down from my higher self, illuminating my entire head and body. For a brief moment, I was engulfed in an energetic ball of this luminous energy. Seconds later, the orbit of my consciousness spiraled out of my body, and as it did, the boundary of my being ballooned in size. Once this expansion reached its limit, I merged with the globe of consciousness surrounding the planet that evolutionary philosopher Pierre Teilhard de Chardin called the *noösphere*.

Right away I knew I was experiencing a planetary level of awareness. Reams of information flooded into my consciousness through an overlay of visionary perceptions and noetic realizations, all revealing the impact of enlightenment on a collective scale.

The initial impression was a profound sense of delight, which came from appreciating the inherent joy all human beings will feel once we collectively reach this stage in our evolution. Related to this was another impression that was far more overwhelming. So much so, in fact, that it thrusted my whole being into a state of shock.

The reason for this overwhelming response came from realizing the fact that once we reach this stage in our collective evolution, we will be far more capable of manifesting our experiences in reality, not just individually, but collectively, as well.

This particular ability was only one of many impressions that were received simultaneously (increased telepathic sensing, greater empathy, and more synchronistic flow were some others), but it alone was enough to grok how radically our entire modus operandi as a species will be altered.

The overall impression was so huge, so revolutionary, and so far from the current level of human development that I wondered if we would ever be capable of evolving our consciousness to such an epic degree. Bravery. That was the most important quality. Whether we'll be fearless enough as a species to trust the evolutionary process as it continues to come through us.

In the midst of this revelation, I received another influx of golden light, which flooded my entire being. This time the blast was so bright that I was momentarily blinded.

When my vision returned, a radiant figure that I immediately recognized as Jesus appeared in the center of my mind. At this point, I was no longer in an expanded state of planetary awareness. Instead, I was back inside my body, inwardly witnessing the light emanating from the figure of Jesus, who shone like a golden sun.

My entire head and chest area felt especially lit up, but the same golden glow filled the rest of my body, and also extended beyond it into my aura.

My first impulse was to dismiss the appearance of Jesus as some kind of residual religious content left over in my subconscious mind that hadn't been purified by the transformation I experienced in 1996. But even as I thought about it, I knew there was more to this mystical encounter.

My next thought was that this vision was similar to the flaming blue Buddha that had appeared inwardly while I was in Colombia in 2000. But once again, I knew another explanation was needed. The energy of aliveness emanating from Jesus was so tangible that it felt far more like a visitation from a spiritually living being than a symbolic form of higher consciousness.

To confirm my hunch, I received another vision. Buddha, Lao Tzu, Confucius, Mohammed, and many other significant yet unfamiliar spiritual figures all flashed by. Their faces were contained in frames that scrolled through my mind's eye like a Rolodex.

The message was clear. Each of these enlightened beings had incarnated into the world as **avatars** to advance the spiritual evolution of humanity, and any one of them could have appeared as my messenger. Yet it was Jesus who did, which was perplexing because I'd never really felt an inclination to relate to Jesus, not even during my time with Mr. Michael.

As a result, my childhood resistance re-emerged, and I questioned whether Jesus was an avatar, a great teacher, or simply a good man. Finally, to verify both his divine status as an avatar and to help me better understand the purpose of his life, I was granted one more vision, this time of Jesus' death.

I saw drops of blood dripping from his dying body on the cross, and as his blood sank into the earth, I knew that when Jesus was being crucified, he vowed to remain available in the spirit world, along with other **ascended masters**, in order to help guide and assist the evolution of humanity.

From beginning to end this entire mystical experience only lasted about ten seconds or so, but the overall impact was so powerful that the transformational effects continued long after the visions and revelations ended.

During the next few weeks, powerful forces flowed into my being from Jesus. As a result, all the enthusiasm I was supposed to have felt during my childhood was fully aroused. My heart was brimming with unconditional love and trust, making it feel completely natural and easy to revere Jesus in the most devotional way.

Throughout this period, I felt the mystical presence of Jesus permeating my entire being, filling it with spiritual light and other divine energies that I soon discovered could be shared with others.

I had just begun teaching in public when the first transmission occurred. I was giving talks every Sunday at the time. The format was a brief meditation period followed by an inspired teaching.

I had been inviting people in attendance to meditate with their eyes open as a way of cultivating the liberating perspective of witnessing at all times. During the group meditation, I received another influx of golden light just as I had before, only this time it came down in a more continuous way. It poured into my body through my crown chakra and shone out of my third eye like a magnified laser beam. I immediately started looking at people, especially those who had their eyes open, eager to see if it was possible to funnel any of this spiritual energy into them.

It seemed to work. After the meditation ended, I asked people for feedback, not mentioning the phenomenon I'd just witnessed to avoid influencing anyone's response. Several people shared that they felt noticeable shifts occur in their awareness, and one woman, unable to express herself using words, was weeping in gratitude and communicating with her eyes that she had experienced a cathartic release of deep emotional pain.

Teaching after the light began descending

Encouraged by these results, I continued to explore my ability to share this luminous energy with others, remaining both secretive about my experiments and critically detached to ensure that I wasn't deluding myself or anyone else.

Golden light as well as some new energies started coming down during the group meditation period, which ushered in an exciting phase in my spiritual development.

During these transmissions, I started noticing how these luminous energies filled people's auras with other colors in addition to gold. Most notably, silver, white, red, blue, and black. The subtle bodies described in many esoteric teachings also began appearing during these transmissions. And in certain individuals, these energetic layers would sometimes coalesce and form a single, radiant **light body**.

Soon after this development, several people reported seeing a similar light body outshining my physical form, and one person described an energetic vortex hovering above my head, attended by many beings of light all weaving vortexes over everyone else's head in attendance.

Meanwhile, temporary spiritual awakenings were occurring in many of the people in attendance, and more than once the entire group realized the same level of nondual awareness simultaneously.

It didn't take very long for me to realize that my ability to share these divine energies with others was an effective way to help individuals and groups awaken their true nature. It did, however, take a few years for me to better understand and stabilize my ability to work with them.

Also, the process of discovering the full extent of their effects is still unfolding. One of the features of these energies is that they are constantly revealing new information about what they can be used for and how to continue working with them. What follows is a summary of the main qualities and actions of each energy according to their color.

Golden light is the energy of creation. It comes from the dimension that first emerged when God said, "Let there be light." When descending freely, this energy gushes down like golden mist laced with hues of silver and white light. At first, it gathers into a pool of unformed energy before congealing into the various forms of reality. The main effect of this light is that it awakens the soul's ability to realize various truths, such as the oneness of everything, the same self everywhere, matter as energy, and so forth. It can also cause both manifesting and synchronicity to increase in one's life.

Black light is the energy of pre-creation. It comes from the unmanifested realm of existence before God said, "Let there be light." Although this primordial energy lacks color, it has a distinct quality that is just as perceptible as the other energies. When it descends, it is like a shadow that momentarily eclipses the ordinary perception of reality. The primary effect of this energy is that it removes all the layers of egoic identification, revealing our true nature.

Red light is a specific energy that works on grounding true nature in the body, allowing a person to be in the world without feeling separate from spirit. When it descends, it has a healing effect that makes it easier to let go of negative emotions, which aids in the removal of past karmas. It also has a density that makes it feel heavier and more substantial than the other energies.

Blue light is another quality of these energies that works specifically on illuminating and enlightening the mind. Its presence is very subtle and cool, similar to the soft blue light of the daytime sky. When it descends, it facilitates the shift in consciousness beyond ego by revealing that the essence of the mind is pure consciousness. This, in turn, allows the clear light of the witnessing soul to emerge, which, again, leads to the realization of our true nature.

Clear light is the other main energy that can descend. When it does, it widens the boundary of the self beyond all limits, leading to direct experiences of nondual being. Like all the other energies, clear light can be seen. It looks similar to daylight, except that it is more ethereal than physical light.

So, that's a basic summary of the qualities, actions, and effects of these energies. Over the years, I have shared these energies with hundreds of individuals. In addition to realizing their true nature, people have reported results such as improved mood, more energy, greater clarity of mind, feelings of inner peace and unconditional love, enhanced intuitions, increased synchronicities, and a profound sense of connectedness with all life. People have even reported cures or improvements in severe and chronic health conditions. And improvements in other areas such as relationships, business, and finances have also been reported.

As a final note, these energies can descend one at a time or in various combinations. When flowing freely, they create two corresponding spiral-shaped whorls that form an hourglass shape around the body. This toroidal energy pattern funnels the higher energies downwards from above and then upwards from below in a feedback loop that fills the aura.

As these gathering energies grow in intensity, they begin pulsing and breathing. Then, at a certain point, the influx of these energies becomes so strong that they illuminate the light body, which is a powerful way to bring these energies more fully into one's own life and the world.

Again, there are parallels for all the experiences described above. For example, mystics, monks, saints, and laypeople have been reporting visions and personal interactions with Jesus throughout the centuries. One of the most famous examples is the Apostle Paul, who was actually dedicated to the persecution of early Christians. According to the book of Acts, his conversion happened after the death of Jesus, who he had never actually met during his lifetime.

Paul was traveling from Jerusalem to Damascus when Jesus appeared to him in a vision of great light and told him to go into the city and wait. The encounter left Paul blind for three days. Meanwhile, in a subsequent vision, Jesus appeared to one of his followers, Ananias, who lived in Damascus, and told him where to find Paul in order to restore his sight by the laying of hands. The experience transformed Paul into such an ardent believer in the divinity of Jesus that he became one of the most influential early Christian missionaries.

While some seekers may be inclined to dismiss the possibility of supernatural encounters with ascended masters outright, or place less significance on them spiritually, it is important to realize that, although quite rare, they do happen. To understand how these kinds of encounters are possible, it helps to put them into a broader, more comprehensive context, one that describes the big picture.

According to most esoteric cosmologies, reality consists of three major realms: the causal, the subtle, and the physical. The causal realm refers to the boundless dimension of energy prior to manifestation and is associated with the experience of formless awareness found in deep meditation. The physical realm refers to the material universe and is associated with the experience of waking consciousness. And in between is the subtle realm, which is comprised of various nonphysical planes of existence and is associated with dreaming, astral travel, and the afterlife. Altogether, these three realms make up the entire spectrum of reality, which begins with the formless energy of God manifesting into denser and more material planes of existence.

The subtle realm is where the human soul usually goes after physical death, and includes the various heavens, hells, purgatories, limbos, bardo realms, ancestor worlds, and so forth, as recorded in the sacred texts of the world. Religious conditioning sometimes creates fears about being punished in the afterlife, but these beliefs are based on a misunderstanding of the spirit world.

All afterlife phenomena occur as subjective co-creations of the human soul interacting within the mercurial environment of the subtle realm, which is designed for the purpose of reviewing past lives and preparing for future ones in order to make progress on the journey to enlightenment. It is only because the life review can be distressing for some souls that accounts of hell are sometimes reported by people who come close to death and have an unpleasant experience.

In contrast, people who have positive near-death experiences generally report entering a luminous dimension that matches the heavenly paradise described in the religion of that person, primarily to meet their expectations before going through the life review.

Regardless of the different features, most souls spend a certain amount of time in the subtle realm between physical incarnations to resolve their karma. This afterlife period may also include brief experiences in the causal realm before incarnating into another physical body to start a new life.

However, in the case of more highly evolved souls, such as saints, sages, bodhisattvas, and buddhas, a slightly different outcome is achieved. These ascended masters are able to move through the subtle realm quickly and easily and reach the highest realization of the causal realm – the I AM Presence – which is a complete unity with God.

Traditionally, this level of self-realization is said to end the cycle of reincarnation, but my understanding is that while most spiritually advanced souls can remain in the causal or the subtle realms for longer periods (indefinitely if they choose), many (if not all) decide to physically incarnate from time to time in order to help bring other human beings back to God and to work towards the enlightenment of the world.

In fact, according to many New Age teachings, there have been, and will be, many instances of ascended masters incarnating on Earth for this very reason. And to bring this discussion full circle, another one of the ways ascended masters can assist us from the spirit world is by imparting spiritual abilities to embodied human beings the way Jesus did with me.

In terms of the existence of the light body, it is well documented in both new and old traditions. In addition to being known as the light body in the New Age worldview, it is also known as the *glorified body* in Christianity, the *diamond body* in Taoism, and the *rainbow body* in Tibetan Buddhism, to name a few. John White, an internationally known author and educator in the fields of consciousness research and higher human development, has compiled a list of comparable terms from many other traditions.[7]

It should be mentioned that not all of these traditions regard the light body in the same way, or even as serving the same function. Each tradition has its own methods, goals, and teachings, and they are not always the same from one to the next. However, that the light body has been observed and recorded in various spiritual traditions the world over is a clear testament to its universality as a phenomenological reality.

Stated briefly, we humans have an energetic field or spiritual body that is composed of several layers and chakras that create the aura surrounding and permeating our physical forms. These layers and chakras are involved in processing all kinds energies, from basic sensations to spiritual bliss. What's more, it's possible to learn how to channel the highest and holiest of energies for the purpose of enlightening life on Earth, which, when done well, illuminates the spiritual body.

Lastly, in terms of drawing the necessary energies down into the world to advance our spiritual evolution, one of the most pronounced approaches is found in Kabbalah, the mystical tradition within Judaism. According to Kabbalists, the true role of humanity is to *divinize* the world, and, ultimately, all of creation. Kabbalists work towards this goal by meditating on the golden light and other divine energies above the head, drawing these spiritual forces down into the world to effect individual, collective, global, and cosmic transformation.

Channeling these divine energies is the final method in this book. This is a skill that only advanced adepts should attempt to cultivate. It takes a great deal of selflessness and careful training to develop and sustain this ability, and there are potential problems and pitfalls that can occur along the way.

The biggest risk is channeling subtle negative forces that delight in bringing harm and destruction into the human realm. This is a particular challenge for unenlightened seekers at an immature level of personal and mystical development, who may not be able to discern and therefore stop these deceptive influences from coming through.

Another risk is ego inflation. This usually happens when a person is unprepared to properly handle the expansion of awareness and energy that goes along with developing this ability. Our consciousness naturally inflates as we spiral upwards into the higher self and our souls are infused with holy energies when we're channeling. A problem can occur when the ego seizes upon this activity and uses it to feel superior or special. Humility and gratitude counteract this tendency. It also helps to remember that when these energies are flowing through you, it is not your doing but rather grace from God.

The shaded box on the following page explains how to channel energy. Doing it safely hinges on being aware of the associated spiritual dangers and carefully learning to become both a clear vessel and an effective conduit.

Channeling Energy
Bless the space with a simple prayer of your design and order all lower entities and negative forces to leave if they are around. Call on any spirit guides or masters who work with you to come and assist. Even if you don't see or sense them, trust that they'll be there. Just ask for the "highest and the best" to help you. Next, raise your vibration until you completely merge with your higher self. When you're ready, shape your consciousness into a tube that extends down into your body. Once this pathway is set in place, hold it open until it's clear and unwavering. If you remain concentrated in this way long enough, divine light and other spiritual energies may come through you for your own benefit as well as for others, the world, and beyond.

So there you have it, the final method of this book, as well as the conclusion of my autobiography. There are more details and experiences I could share from my journey, but I'll leave it here for now. Before finishing, though, I would like to share a few closing remarks.

Hopefully the authenticity of my account speaks for itself, but in case there is any doubt about the purity of my motivation, I'd just like to state that I have absolutely no interest in being glorified or exploiting people's spiritual longing for my own benefit. My only desire is to serve God by guiding other souls back home. Being a guru is not a role I sought out. The only reason I accepted this sacred duty is because I've always known that it's my destiny, which was confirmed when God asked me to tell others about my awakening.

With that said, I sincerely hope that I've expressed enough to answer my calling and to humbly convey that the purpose of my life is to assist others on the path. To that end, my deepest wish is that the teachings and techniques in this book help you on your journey, and furthermore, that they contribute to the spiritual awakening of humanity.

Autobiographical Summary

M Y SPIRITUAL JOURNEY began in early infancy with a recurring metamorphosis of consciousness that was experienced every night and which continued throughout childhood. A sequence of other mystical states of awareness and out-of-body experiences also occurred from a young age that helped maintain an almost uninterrupted connection to the formless dimension of being.

This constant recognition of the source and substance of everyone and everything in existence was accompanied by the knowledge that the purpose of my life was to maintain and ultimately share this realization of oneness with others.

Upon entering adolescence, I deliberately chose to relinquish my access to this level of self-realization, knowing in advance that I would eventually rediscover and fully embody it once again in adulthood.

After the decision was made at the start of adolescence to forget about the absolute truth, a series of events then followed that inspired my search to rediscover it once again.

This search eventually culminated in a direct encounter with the very source of existence, which completely changed my life in early adulthood, marking a permanent shift in my consciousness beyond ego.

In the midst of this psychospiritual conversion, I received a calling to tell others about the ultimate nature of reality, which reminded me that it is my destiny to help seekers awaken and fully realize their true nature.

This spiritual transformation occurred in 1996, but I didn't discuss it with anyone until many years later, mainly because there was no language or context to describe it until then. The intervening years were dedicated to fully integrating my true nature and getting ready to guide others on the path.

The first few years were spent stabilizing the transcendental level of self-realization, followed by several more years to complete the grounding phase, with this entire period defined by the dual challenge of comprehending what had occurred and finding a way to communicate it clearly.

Meanwhile, more unusual phenomena, supernatural incidents, and significant processes and realizations continued occurring, all of which had to be integrated and then understood conceptually so that these developments could be communicated, as well.

Finally, in 2006, soon after I began offering teachings on the process of spiritual awakening and the evolutionary destiny of humanity, I went through another transformation that led to my ability to bring divine energies down into the world, making them more accessible to others.

During the process of developing this ability, I realized that it represented the highest function I could perform in life to help others awaken their true nature, as well as contribute to the collective awakening of humanity. Through this work, my goal is to keep liberating people and pushing the spiritual evolution of the planet forward.

Multidimensional Map of Reality

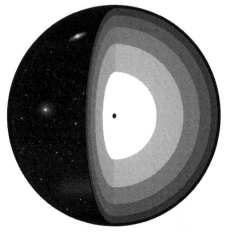

This diagram is a basic model of the universe. The black dot at the center represents the causal realm, which is the unmanifested source of existence. This is the primordial dimension at the heart of creation. Although it is the smallest feature in this diagram, it is actually the largest dimension imaginable. So large, in fact, that it is beyond measurement. It is not only infinite in size, but eternal in age, as well. This is the mysterious origin of the universe that we call by name God.

Extending outward from this formless realm is a luminous realm of pure creative light, represented by the white band in the diagram. This dimension is God's first act of creation, and without it, no other forms or forces could exist in the universe. It turns the unmanifested source of existence into a substance suitable for all manifestation to occur. This is the same light we see in our material universe, but at this original level of reality it exists in a totally fluidic state similar to plasma. To be precise, it is a luminous and intelligent web interwoven with innumerable strings of energy that turn God's causal ideations into all the vibrating forms of creation, both seen and unseen.

Between this original light and the physical universe is the subtle realm, which is the nonphysical dimension of reality where God's creative light first manifests into visible forms. It is represented by the shaded bands of grey to illustrate the decreasing luminosity and increasing density of reality as you approach the physical, as well as to show that there are levels in this realm. In the narrative, I grouped these levels together as the various religious descriptions of the afterlife.

What I didn't mention is that every soul ends up at whatever level best matches their current state of spiritual evolution, and while gloomy places exist where lost or tormented souls go through periods of intense reflection, the majority of the subtle realm is vibrant with God's creative light. This gives all the inhabitants the ability to alter their environments any way they please, although karmic requirements are present to ensure that the upper regions remain heavenly. Yet even the most beautiful places imaginable are not the ultimate source of liberation. Only when the soul attains a complete and lasting union with God in the causal realm is final freedom found.

The physical dimension is represented by the black outer band, which is the end result in this continuum of cosmic energy vibrating into denser forms of matter. A little-known fait accompli is that the material universe was created by God so that beings like us could evolve and eventually awaken while embodied in physical forms. Being both the densest and farthest from the source of existence makes it the most difficult realm to awaken in, which is precisely what makes it the most rewarding. We fulfill God's deepest yearning when our souls awaken while physically incarnated as human beings.

In sum, the incredible state of absolute nothingness lies at the end of our journey as the ultimate spiritual goal as well as being the origin from which all things begin.

Overview of Exercises

The key to making progress spiritually is to find a group of effective techniques and then use them consistently. The nine practices in this book are all methods I've used and benefited from on my journey. I've also refined these methods for over a decade working as a spiritual teacher with people from all walks of life. The result is a collection of practices that catalyze enlightened states of consciousness. It is my hope that one, some, or all of them will be helpful on your journey. Here's a quick breakdown.

Self-Observation and Focusing Attention are preliminary practices that help build the skills needed to use more direct methods to awaken and realize your true nature.

Tracing Back the Witness and Mirror Gazing are the two most direct methods I know of. They provide good glimpses of nondual awareness and take seconds to perform once you get the hang of them.

The Sonic Truth and Yantra Meditations are classic practices found in many spiritual traditions, and either one can be very effective in turning those temporary glimpses into a permanent gaze if practiced daily.

The Sensing Meditation is great for post-awakening integration because it helps ground one's realization in the body and the world, but it's also a useful preliminary practice.

And finally, Channeling Energy is an advanced method for people who want to help bring about a collective awakening in human consciousness. It isn't suitable for people who are still trying to realize and stabilize their true nature.

However, along the way, the Quantum Gazing exercise is a great way to develop the perceptual abilities needed to possibly channel energy one day.

Mystical Poems

The following selection of poems are inspired by significant experiences from my spiritual journey in the order they happened, forming a poetic version of my autobiography.

Poetry is an especially effective form of literature for expressing mystical realizations in words. If you're open to receiving it, mystical poetry can give your soul a taste of whatever spiritual reality or truth the poem is about.

What's more, similar to the beneficial effects from singing hymns or chanting mantras, reading mystical poetry can produce changes in your consciousness that assist the awakening process.

DIVINE SPARK

Hidden within is an inner sun
That first emerges like a distant star.
This speck of light small as a quark
Gathers energy from God's eternal night
Until it shines like an ocean of light.

You hold in your core this atomic fleck
Born from the formless before the big bang
And woven with billions of filaments
That form the fabric of all existence.

SPACECRUISER

for A. H. Almaas

Spiraling down from the firmament fell
A massive bejeweled chandelier
That squeezed itself into my eyes
And landed somewhere deep inside.

There it stayed for about a year
Waiting until I was ready to receive
The crowning acuity transmitted by
This striking form that fell from the sky.

Maybe for you it came as a ufo?
Holy angels sharing sacred words?
Or perhaps some other celestial anatomy
Carrying this blessed information about reality.

For when it arrives, however it may,
Your own personal spacecruiser
Fueled by an ageless alchemy
Levels the peaks and fills the valleys
Letting you hover around the original ground.

THE WORD
for Christopher Dewdney

Impossible words once hovered
in the atmosphere above
our monkey intelligence.

Before the rain of words came down
our primal minds moved constantly
and without the boundary
that so much open space
could be separated
into sounds like
sky & savanna.

We began to play with those verbal angels
condensing our free roaming thoughts
into solid shapes that turned
known oases into named places.

We were magnetized
by the miracle of The Word
holding us higher, together.

We can reach even higher
for another level of language
waiting to descend.

We can learn to sing like shamans
whose icaros reopen the sky
with vowels of infinity
conjuring consonance
into this rambling world.

NIRVANA
for Ken Wilber

When God's consciousness reinstalls
It forces the dismantling of our walls
And strips the self with a devouring hand
Leaving us naked with no place to stand
Upon a groundless ground made of energy
Where we merge and meet our true identity.

Even the trail of our journey's steps
Disappear in this almighty eclipse.
A blissful emptiness replaces our vacancy
That dreams of a life filled with felicity.

Freed from the ego's karmic needs
Replaced by love's eternal ease
And the burning desire that our souls release
What the divine on earth wants to unleash
In waves that make all our activity
An endless expression of heaven's harmony.

Descending from these timeless peaks
Are fount-filled angels made to reach
Our human need to blissfully release
Into this life an evolving peace.

AFTERLIFE

Arriving from this earthly plane
our ascending souls do go
into a realm more malleable
where thoughts become reality
and everything that appears
has an element of our psyches
mirrored back for us to see.

When we first arrive
we review our lives
as if it were a show.

Some stand before a council of elders
while others see a judge and jury
or perhaps a more modern anomaly
like watching a movie summarizing
your entire life instantaneously.

If you're able to observe things purely
God or your guides will lift your soul
into one of many subtler realms
all progressively free from the suffering
that makes our growth down here
seem so painfully slow.

If you're scared of dying and holding on
hungry ghosts or hounds of hell may appear
to tear through your body, biting as they go
until you're ready to leave this world
and shed your embodied ego and identity.

Only then can your life and all your memories
be turned into liberating epiphanies
with enough power to send your soul
soaring through a wormhole
into the transcendent mystery
from which everything endlessly flows.

SONIC TRUTH

for Ram Dass

It's so soft we often miss it
although it's always there.

For some it's like a chirping cricket
calling out in the nighttime air.

For others it comes in less quiet ways
like the crashing of the ocean's waves.

Eventually you'll hear a chandelier
dangling from your inner ear.

This most pleasing of sounds
comes from a stillness without bounds.

With a message containing the following refrain:
From formless oneness the cosmos came.

To find this sonic truth in you
listen for this subtle cue:

It begins as OM then rises as HU
until everything's one and there's no more you.

SOLAR VISION
for Aurobindo

This body is a vessel of light
Capable of channeling Creation's sight
That brings a rapture so divinely sweet
Where love alone is all we meet.

God's golden light widens this cage
Into a circumference both vast and vague
That makes the world throb with ecstasy
In pulsing thrills arousing eternity.

O boundless heartbeat made of stardust
How is it that you beat in us?

Glossary

Absolute truth refers to the ultimate nature of everything in existence as a manifestation of the formless dimension.

Angels are divine beings created by God to assist all souls in the awakening and ascension process.

Ascended master is a realized being who serves humanity from the spirit world and occasionally incarnates into the physical world as an avatar.

Astral projection is a form of out-of-body experience (OBE) in which the spiritual body separates from the physical body and travels in the astral plane or subtle realm, with the possibility of reaching the causal realm (enlightenment), at which point the spiritual body is dropped.

Aura is the energy field surrounding living beings.

Avatar is a Sanskrit term meaning "crosses down" or "one who descends." It refers to the deliberate incarnation of an ascended master or realized being into the world in order to further the evolution of consciousness and civilization.

Chakra is a Sanskrit term meaning "center" or "wheel." They are subtle energy centers in and around the body that funnel energies specific to the human experience.

Collective unconscious is a term coined by Carl Jung to refer to the reservoir of ancestral traits accumulated by the human species over the course of its evolution.

Enlightenment is a direct encounter with the source of existence, called, depending on the tradition, *Brahman*, *Tao*, *Nirvana*, *God*, and so forth.

Epiphany is a sudden and striking realization that leads to a deeper perspective or breakthrough in understanding, also known as an 'aha' moment.

Guru is a Sanskrit term for a spiritual teacher or master who embodies the enlightened condition and is also a channel for divine grace and energy.

Higher self is the part of our being that connects us to God. It is located about a foot and a half above the head.

Inner guide is the still, small voice within that always knows what's best for us and also leads the soul home. It comes from the higher self, which is our direct channel to God.

Integral Theory is a comprehensive approach to understanding all the dimensions of reality, developed by Ken Wilber.

Karma refers to the collection of credits and debits based on previous actions that influence the kinds of conditions encountered in life.

Koan is a paradoxical anecdote or riddle used in Zen Buddhism to provoke enlightenment. A well-known example is the question, "What is the sound of one hand clapping?"

Kundalini is an energy that exists at the base of the spine, usually in a dormant state. When aroused, it moves up the spine, opening each of the chakras along the way, until reaching the crown chakra, which liberates the soul from the body so that it can merge with the higher self.

Light body refers to the spiritual illumination of the human energy field or spiritual body, which is activated through a combination of personal effort and divine grace.

Mandala is a form of sacred art used in various traditions to foster spiritual growth and transformation.

Mantra is a method of spiritual practice that involves chanting sacred sounds.

New Age is a Western spiritual movement that developed in the second half of the twentieth century and includes practices and philosophies from new and old traditions alike.

Nondual is a translation of the Sanskrit term *advaita*, which means "not two." It refers to the unity of the world of form and the formless dimension, as well as the awareness of this truth as a direct perception.

Perennial philosophy is a set of core truths and teachings common to all the world's great wisdom traditions, with the attainment of self-realization forming a central feature.

Phenomenology is the study of "phenomena," or things as they appear in consciousness. It emphasizes the subjective or first person point of view as a valid mode of knowing about the quality or nature of direct experience.

Self-realization refers to the discovery that one's true self is the timeless, boundless, and formless bliss of pure being.

Soul is the part of us that evolves and grows from one incarnation to the next. It is equivalent to consciousness, with the added understanding that our consciousness can also exist independently from the physical body.

Soul companions are kindred spirits who stay together over many lifetimes out of mutual love and respect and often share several past-life connections.

Spirit guides are disincarnate spirits who can act as guides to incarnated human beings.

Spirit world refers to the subtle dimension where all souls go between physical incarnations to rest and reflect between lives, and to get support and guidance on the journey to final enlightenment and full self-realization.

Tantra is a nondual spiritual movement that originated in India during the early medieval period and is expressed in scriptures called *Tantras*. The term comes from two Sanskrit root words, *tanoti* (expansion of awareness or consciousness) and *trayati* (liberation of energy).

Theosophical Society is an organization that formed in 1875 and is still active today. It was largely responsible for the dissemination of esoteric and occult knowledge in the West during the twentieth century, and it also contributed many components to the New Age movement.

True nature is the formless essence at the core of our being. It is experienced as the primordial source and dynamically evolving substance of everything in existence, which awakens the nondual view that reality is one indivisible unity.

Endnotes

1. Wikipedia contributors, "Third Eye." *Wikipedia, The Free Encyclopedia*, accessed July 23, 2012.

2. Almaas, A. H. *Spacecruiser Inquiry: True Guidance for the Inner Journey*. Shambhala, 2002, pg. 216.

3. Goldman, Jonathan. "Chakra Chants" essay in accompanying booklet. Spirit Music, 1999. Compact disc.

4. Wikipedia contributors, "Transpersonal Chakras." *Wikipedia, The Free Encyclopedia*, accessed September 24, 2012.

5. Wikipedia contributors, "Subpersonal Chakras." *Wikipedia, The Free Encyclopedia*, accessed September 24, 2012.

6. Hawkins, David R. *Discovery of the Presence of God: Devotional Nonduality*. Veritas Publishing, 2006, pg. 238–9.

7. White, John. "Resurrection and the Body of Light." *Quest* Volume 97 #1: 11–15, Winter 2009.

An Open Invitation

The spiritual path is a lifelong journey of awakening, exploration, discovery, healing, and increasing joy. For many, reading books, listening to teachings, and watching videos is a great way to stay motivated. But along the way, many seekers eventually recognize the need for more personal guidance. And the truth is, without the personal guidance of a spiritual teacher or guru, fully awakening and integrating one's true nature is unlikely for all but the most keen and gifted. Ever since my awakening, I've been transmitting the enlightened state of being to others and skillfully guiding seekers on their journey to full self-realization. If you'd like to experience how working with me can help you fully awaken your true nature, I encourage you to get in touch with me through my website.

www.stephendamico.com

Made in the USA
San Bernardino, CA
05 July 2018